NEW MEXICO
KICKS ON

ROUTE
66

TEXT BY MARTIN LINK
PHOTOGRAPHS BY LARRY LINDAHL

RIO NUEVO
PUBLISHERS

UTAH

COLORADO

NEW MEXICO

ARIZONA

TEXAS

Navajo Indian Reservation

CHACO CULTURE NATIONAL HISTORIC PARK

KASHA-KATUWE TENT ROCKS NATIONAL MONUMENT

(491) **Gallup**

Red Rock State Park

Continental Divide

Thoreau

KEWA (SANTO DOMINGO) PUEBLO

Santa Fe

Glorieta

Pecos

Las Vegas

(84)

Romeroville

Conchas Lake

Ute Reservoir

(54)

(602)

FORT WINGATE

Mt. Taylor

Budville

Paraje

(44)

Bernalillo

Sandia Crest

(25)

(285)

PECOS NATIONAL HISTORIC PARK

Dilia

Pecos River

Glenrio

Zuni Indian Reservation

(53)

Milan

Grants

McCartys

Laguna

Mesita

(14)

Albuquerque

(84)

Tucumcari

Cuervo

Rio Grande

EL MORRO NATIONAL MONUMENT

EL MALPAIS NATIONAL MONUMENT

ACOMA PUEBLO

(40)

Tijeras

ISLETA PUEBLO

Edgewood

Moriarty

Clines Corners

(84)

(40)

San Jon

(6)

Los Lunas

Santa Rosa

(25)

(285)

(84)

Lake Sumner

Vaughn

(60)

Fort Sumner

Legend
▬▬▬	I-40 & Route 66 overlap
▬▬▬	Historic Route 66
▬▬▬	Route 66 prior to 1937

Above: 1923 Ford Model T and Route 66 postcard, "The Plaza, Old Laguna" from the Cibola Arts Council Double Six Gallery. **Below:** Relief from the Santa Rosa Courthouse.

CONTENTS

INTRODUCTION

IT'S A GOOD OLD ROAD, our Route 66, which over the years has become a national and international legend through popular culture and the arts, including literature, film, music, and television. This "Mother Road," from its opening in 1926 to its decommissioning as a U.S. highway in October, 1984, played a prominent role in transforming the nation.

In 1875, a serious appeal for better roads made the news, and it came from what today seems like a very unlikely source—the nation's growing population of bicycle riders. In 1880, East Coast bicyclists organized into the League of American Wheelmen, which shortly thereafter became a national organization.

Their lobbying efforts for good roads soon involved farmers from throughout the South and Midwest, and the farmers' own national advocacy group, The Grange, joined forces with the Wheelmen. They contended that improved rural roads would allow farmers to transport their produce, especially vegetables, to urban markets on a more timely schedule. And the idea of free delivery of rural mail was also becoming a popular subject. In 1891, the Wheelmen published "The Gospel of Good Roads: A Letter to American Farmers."

In 1892, more than 1,000 bicycle fans gathered in Chicago

Top: High Wheel Bicycle Club, circa 1885.

Above: Membership card to the League of American Wheelmen.

Right: Charles E. Duryea in the automobile he and his brother Frank invented, circa 1893.

and organized the National League of Good Roads. They elected General Roy Stone, an engineer and Civil War hero, as secretary. Their objective: national road legislation.

At the Chicago World's Fair: Columbian Exposition in 1893, hundreds of road-hungry individuals, along with colleges, trade unions, and The Grange, held demonstrations and called for government action. The bicyclists were soon joined by car owners. That same year, the first American-built automobile, the Duryea, was exhibited at the Exposition and made quite a hit.

The Secretary of Agriculture created the Office of Road Inquiry (ORI) as a first step in building hard-surfaced highways for the country, and named General Stone to head up the new organization. Stone's mission was to evaluate the nation's cross-country roads and investigate the materials and technology needed to build better ones. In 1900, the ORI and several other road groups met and reorganized themselves into the National Good Roads Association. Even the railroads supported the roads movement, because they could increase their freight business if farmers could get their produce and livestock to the rail lines more easily.

By 1910, as the mass-produced Ford Model T hit the road, every state (and the territories of New Mexico and Arizona) had a National Good Roads Association affiliate.

In 1910, thirty state and national organizations met in Washington, D.C., and formed the American Highway Association.

But it wasn't until the 1920s that the bulk of the population finally decided to turn their horses out to pasture and "afford a Ford," or take Lucille for a "ride in my merry Oldsmobile." Or they purchased a General Motors vehicle that was good "for every purse or purpose," or a Chrysler Imperial, "the car of tomorrow." In 1900, there had been approximately 8,000 autos on U.S. roads. By 1905, there were 77,000, and by 1920, there were nearly 8,000,000—one car for every thirteen people in a nation with a population of 106 million.

Our attention now focuses on Oklahoma. In 1912, the Tulsa County Good Roads Association secretary, Cyrus "Cy" Avery, invited members of Good Roads Associations in Kansas and Texas to a barbeque and business meeting to create a new north-south highway. The Mid-Continental Highway Association was born, and Cyrus Avery was elected secretary. From that day until his retirement fifty years later, Cy Avery was totally enmeshed in creating a transcontinental road that would go from point A to point B, just as long as it went through Tulsa.

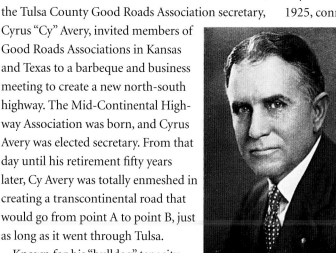

Known for his "bulldog" tenacity and boundless energy, Avery became a member of a number of road associations, and was elected or appointed to various positions, including Chairman of the Oklahoma Highway Commission. In the days before air travel, his attendance at meetings throughout the country was impressive. He'd be at a meeting in Los Angeles at the beginning of the week, and show up at a conference in New Jersey at the end of the week.

His biggest challenge was that most Good Roads Associations and state and local road commissioners were only interested in developing better roads in their county or voting district. Whether nationally supported roads should be thoroughfares only for locals, or were cross-country travel routes connecting the East and West coasts for freight, tourists, and migrants, was a battle that lasted more than two decades.

In 1924, Avery was recruited by the new U.S. Bureau of Public Roads to help with the creation of a national grid system of interstate, regional highways. Avery worked with a committee throughout 1925, connecting hundreds of roads. However, his personal goal was to develop a thoroughfare of existing roads, beginning in Chicago, running through his home state of Oklahoma, and continuing to Los Angeles, California. This unconventional routing violated the accepted grid system and was not well received. The eastern portion, Chicago to Tulsa, was generally oriented north-south, while the remainder of the proposed route, from Tulsa to Los Angeles, competed with other east-west routes. It took months of persuasion by a determined Avery.

About the time that his proposed route won acceptance, a new disagreement arose, this time over the numbering. The U.S. Bureau of Public Roads had created a numbering system that would replace

Vintage autos galore at the fabulous Lewis Antique Auto and Toy Museum in Moriarty.

Left: *Good Roads* Magazine, Number 1, January 1892.

Below: Cyrus Stevens Avery, the "father" of Route 66.

the system of giving routes actual names. In January 1925, the Secretary of Agriculture appointed Avery to the Joint Board to Number Highways (JBNH). In April 1925, the members met for the first time and accepted the official U.S. shield as a good highway marker. By October, the committee had given seventy-six numbers to what would become major highways on 75,884 miles of roads. The road that linked Chicago to Tulsa and Los Angeles was designated U.S. 60.

Governor Fields of Kentucky demanded that the route that started in Newport News, Virginia, and traversed the state of Kentucky should be connected to Springfield, Missouri, and be designated U.S. 60. This would create a true east-west transcoastal highway. The section of Avery's route between Chicago and Springfield, Missouri, would then be labeled U.S. 62. But Cyrus Avery would have none of it! For more than six months, various committees, delegations, and officials joined the controversy. Eventually, Avery asked his highway engineer John Page to look into the numbers that were left over. Page reported that there were still twenty-four unused numbers and that the number 66 might work. Avery thought that was a good choice and recognized that the double sixes was considered a master number in numerology, known to bring material pleasures and success. On April 30, 1926, Avery sent a telegram to Thomas McDonald, Chief of the American Association of State Highway Officials (AASHO): "Regarding Chicago–Los Angeles Road, if California, Arizona, New Mexico, Texas and Illinois will accept Sixty-Six instead of Sixty we are willing to agree to this change. We prefer Sixty-Six to Sixty-Two."

In Washington, D.C., officials received the telegram with elation. The long stalemate was over, and legislation for a national highway system could now be presented to Congress. Getting the final approval of the other five affected states took a while, and the Kentucky delegation was still not happy. But on November 11, 1926, the AASHO members voted to accept the work of the joint board and executive committee. The United States now had a 96,626-mile numbered highway system, and 2,448 of those miles were identified as U.S. 66.

Today, generations of people throughout this country know Cy Avery, if not by name, then by his legacy. More than anything else, he was the father of U.S. Highway 66.

ROUTE 66 NEW MEXICO FACTS

Route 66 underwent more changes and realignments in New Mexico than in any other state.

Route 66 intersects Route 66 at the corner of 4th Street and Central Avenue in downtown Albuquerque.

From 1926 to 1937, Route 66 went through the oldest state capital in the United States, Santa Fe, which was established in 1610. Following realignment, the oldest town on the entire route is Albuquerque, which was established in 1706.

Route 66 passes through three Indian Reservations in New Mexico: Laguna Pueblo, Acoma Pueblo, and the Navajo Reservation.

The original route coincides with the final segment of the historic Santa Fe Trail, and passes through a major Civil War battlefield—the Battle of Glorieta Pass (March 26–28, 1862), sometimes referred to as the "Gettysburg of the West."

The highest point of elevation on the entire Route 66 is the Continental Divide at 7,263 feet (2,214 m).

The only Confederate cemetery on Route 66 is inside the old Cubero cemetery.

Fort Wingate, established just before the Civil War, is one of the oldest and most important forts in the Southwest, and lies on Route 66.

Contact information for many of the establishments listed in this book can be found in the Places to See Along New Mexico's Route 66 section on page 89.

CHAPTER 1

EARLY ROUTE VARIATIONS PRIOR TO 1938

BEFORE NEW MEXICO attained statehood in 1912, it had an active Good Roads Association addressing the monumental task of improving roads. In New Mexico, the first road in what is now the continental United States was laid out in the early 1600s. It was the El Camino Real de Tierra Adentro (The Royal Road of the Interior), linking Santa Fe with Mexico City.

In 1821, a group of Yankee merchants inaugurated a trail from Franklin, Missouri, to Santa Fe, capital of the Spanish-Mexican Provincia de Nuevo Mexico. Within a few years, the trailhead moved to Independence, Missouri, and was improved to accommodate heavy freight wagons. After the Mexican–American War in 1846–1848, both the Camino Real and the western portion of the Santa Fe Trail came under U.S. jurisdiction. Eventually, segments of these historic roads were incorporated into Route 66.

With the achievement of statehood, the politicians and merchants of New Mexico were looking for ways to become more involved with the rest of the country. For the past thirty years, they had concentrated heavily on the development of railroads, but with the introduction of automobiles, interest shifted to roads.

The Good Roads Association identified a proposed route that would enter eastern New Mexico near Tucumcari and continue westward to Santa Rosa. Due to local political pressure, the route then swung northward to Romeroville and incorporated the final sixty-five miles of the historic Santa Fe Trail, past Pecos Ruins and Glorieta Pass, and into

Left: An old gas pump sets the scene in Chimayó, New Mexico.

Right: The infamous La Bajada Hill.

SAM HUDELSON, COURTESY PALACE OF THE GOVERNORS PHOTO ARCHIVES (NMHM/ DCA), 008226.

the state capital. Then it turned south, negotiated La Bajada, and followed the Rio Grande to Albuquerque and Los Lunas.

This left only one segment undecided: The Proposal #1 route would follow the railroad from Albuquerque to Grants and Gallup and then on to Flagstaff, Arizona. The Proposal #2 route would be shorter, with the route going straight from Los Lunas, through Zuni Pueblo, eventually connecting at Holbrook, Arizona. The business people in Gallup and local Indian traders obviously supported Proposal #1.

The New Mexico Good Roads Association met on May 8, 1913, to make the decision. Nineteen delegates were chosen and seventeen of them preferred to show, as an example, that their chosen route was negotiable by automobile.

The seventeen men, divided into four cars, left Gallup before 5:00 a.m. on May 8. Driving time for the 175 miles was 13.5 hours, which averaged thirteen miles per hour. Their escapade seemed to have worked, as the Good Roads Association quickly recommended Proposal #1, the route that followed the Atchison, Topeka and Santa Fe Railway.

During this same time period, the Automobile Club of Southern California (ACSC) was establishing a route from Los Angeles to Williams, Arizona. By the summer of 1913, the only portion still in question was the region between western New Mexico and Williams that paralleled the railroad.

So, on September 12, a 235-mile auto race was organized from Gallup to Williams. There were seven entries, but five dropped out along the way. The winner, in spite of seventeen flat tires, averaged over twenty miles an hour. His prize was $200, but, more important, it was proven that a person could drive an automobile from Albuquerque to Williams, and on to Los Angeles, California.

The next ten years (1913–1923) saw dynamic change for the United States, including the improvement of automobiles and trucks, the introduction of the telephone and radio, and the development of air traffic. One major accomplishment of the New Mexico Highway Department was the modification of the horrendous La Bajada escarpment.

La Bajada (Spanish for "the descent") was part of the original El Camino Real, and dropped over 800 feet in 1.6 miles with twenty-three hairpin switchbacks. All the Highway Department had done thus far was straighten some switchbacks at the upper portion and post a sign reading, in part, "This Road is Not Fool Proof But Safe For a Sane Driver." Cars with gravity-flow fuel systems instead of fuel pumps had to be driven up the hill in reverse to keep the engine running. The nuisance and danger of tight hairpin turns with no edge barriers or any other safety features was daunting. Improvements were finally made in the 1910s–20s, but it was still treacherous. From Santa Fe to Los Lunas, Route

The Rio Puerco bridge, now on the National Register of Historic Places, played an important role in the development of Route 66.

Looking west down Albuquerque's Central Avenue, 1946.

Below: Arthur T. Hannett, New Mexico governor who devised a plan that would become known as Retribution Road.
LIBRARY OF CONGRESS

66 retraced eighty miles of the Spanish colonial El Camino Real.

In November 1926, Route 66 became a reality, and the circuitous 506-mile washboard journey of a number of existing roads were now combined under a single designation: Route 66. Revenge politics then played an important role in the ultimate route of this fledgling highway. So let's back up a couple of years.

In 1923, Governor James Hinkle appointed a Gallup lawyer and former mayor, Arthur T. Hannett, to the State Highway Commission. Toward the end of his first two-year term, Hinkle crossed the politically powerful group known as the "Santa Fe Ring." At the September 1924 Democratic Convention, Hinkle was forced to resign, and Arthur Hannett was nominated as the Democratic candidate. Hannett was elected governor and took office on January 1, 1925.

History repeated itself, and the Santa Fe Ring became dissatisfied with Hannett's performance.

Though Hannett won the nomination for a second term in 1926, the split party allowed Republican Richard C. Dillon to win the election. Infuriated, Hannett came up with a plan to get even with the Santa Fe politicians.

Hannett realized that he had less than two months as a "lame-duck" governor to accomplish a "get-even" scheme. He summoned four men to his office—Robert Cooper and E. B. Bail, both district engineers, and Clyde Tingley and Sam Fulton, both maintenance superintendents. Their mission was to build a seventy-six mile road from Santa Rosa to Moriarty. They tackled the assignment with determination and hurriedly gathered all the available grading equipment. The tractors were mostly World War I Caterpillars in the late stages of dissolution. Certain they would be discharged after the new Republican governor's inauguration, they began implementing Hannett's farewell gesture.

From Santa Rosa to the Palma Post Office, there were no trees, and the crews made good time along that forty-one-mile stretch. The Moriarity crews going east had it a lot tougher. For the first eight miles they had fairly open country, but then encountered a thick piñon pine forest. The next twenty-seven miles were a real challenge as surveyors scouted the path of least resistance. With cables tied to the trees, tractors yanked them out, roots and all. Behind the tractors came the rough graders, followed by the finishing graders.

December turned windy and snowy. Saboteurs fed sugar to the tractor gas tanks. Sand appeared in the engines. The tractor drivers rolled their beds in the snow and slept alongside their machines. Day by day the two crews moved forward and the gap steadily closed. But by Christmas, the eastbound crews were still snarled up in the piñon forest west of Palma.

The new governor, Richard Dillon, took the oath of office on January 1, 1927, and immediately sent out orders to put an end to "Hannett's Joke." But the engineer did not reach the crews until January 3 and by that time "Hannett's Joke" was an accomplished fact. The sixty-nine-mile route was open with automobiles already using it. The new route was identified as NM6 and was a seventy-six-mile shortcut that, best of all, avoided La Bajada Hill.

Route 66 entered Albuquerque from the north

COURTESY OF JOE SONDERMAN

A steel truss bridge across the Rio Puerco of the East resolved the dilemma of going west out of Albuquerque. This 250-foot bridge, seventeen miles west of Albuquerque, was one of the longest single-span bridges in the Southwest.

A shorter alternative called the Laguna Cutoff soon negotiated the sandy stretch of Nine-Mile Hill, traversed the top of a mesa, and then descended into the valley of the Rio Puerco. After crossing the new bridge, it continued west, eliminating seventeen miles from the previous route.

In 1937, Route 66 was officially realigned with the Santa Rosa and Laguna Cut-offs.

on Fourth Street, bisecting the downtown area and continuing south to Bridge Street. The route then went west over the Barelas Bridge and continued on the west side of the Rio Grande, past Isleta Pueblo to Los Lunas.

In 1931, a bridge was constructed over the Rio Grande, so that Central Avenue could expand west of the river. In 1932, a stretch of road a couple miles to the east replaced the switchbacks of La Bajada.

The new route, from the Texas to Arizona borders, was 399 miles long, as compared to the original 506 miles. It removed Santa Fe and Los Lunas from being fully integrated in Route 66 travel and guaranteed a rapid growth of Albuquerque as a tourist center. Prior to this realignment, there were three tourist courts on east Central Avenue. Four years later, there were thirty-seven tourist facilities on both ends of Central Avenue.

The Mother Road had come of age.

Left: The '57 Chevrolet Bel Air owned by James "Bozo" Cordova and displayed inside his Route 66 Auto Museum in Santa Rosa.

Right: The Comet II Drive In & Restaurant in Santa Rosa proudly displays neon and a Route 66 sign that light up at night.

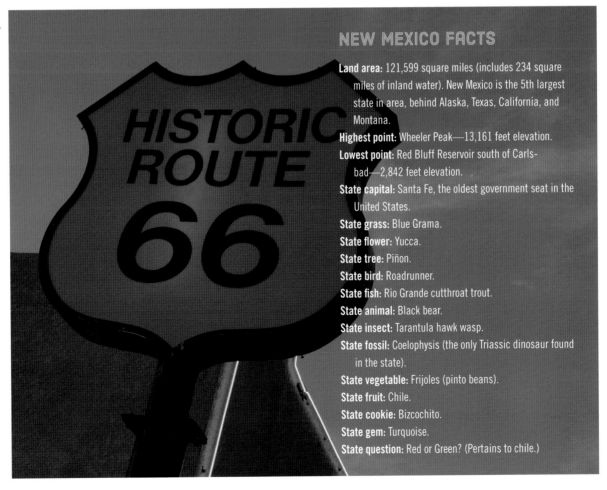

NEW MEXICO FACTS

Land area: 121,599 square miles (includes 234 square miles of inland water). New Mexico is the 5th largest state in area, behind Alaska, Texas, California, and Montana.

Highest point: Wheeler Peak—13,161 feet elevation.

Lowest point: Red Bluff Reservoir south of Carlsbad—2,842 feet elevation.

State capital: Santa Fe, the oldest government seat in the United States.

State grass: Blue Grama.

State flower: Yucca.

State tree: Piñon.

State bird: Roadrunner.

State fish: Rio Grande cutthroat trout.

State animal: Black bear.

State insect: Tarantula hawk wasp.

State fossil: Coelophysis (the only Triassic dinosaur found in the state).

State vegetable: Frijoles (pinto beans).

State fruit: Chile.

State cookie: Bizcochito.

State gem: Turquoise.

State question: Red or Green? (Pertains to chile.)

RANCHERS AND RENEGADES

GLENRIO TO TUCUMCARI TO SANTA ROSA

WE BEGIN OUR JOURNEY across New Mexico by reflecting on the topography of west Texas and eastern New Mexico. At the border, a vast, featureless land extends from horizon to horizon without obstructions of any kind. It is a sea of green grass in the spring, and then brown the rest of the year, except when occasionally covered by snow in the winter. It is known as the Llano Estacado, commonly referred to as the Staked Plains.

The Llano Estacado has a long history. Fifteen thousand years ago, Clovis Man hunted mammoths around the ancient lake beds. A thousand years ago, ancestors of the Pueblo people hunted buffalo and antelope, as did the Querechos (eastern Apaches) some five hundred years ago.

Don Francisco Vázquez de Coronado's expedition got thoroughly lost in the region now crossed by Route 66/Interstate 40. In May, 1541, Coronado's men built a bridge across the Pecos River, about ten miles south of present-day Santa Rosa at Puerto de Luna, so that his baggage wagons could cross the river. About eighty miles farther east from the bridge, Coronado wrote in his report, "camine otros cinco dias hasta llegar a Unos llanos Tan sin sena como si esto Vieramos engolfados en la mar" (I traveled another five days until I arrived at some plains so without landmarks that it was as if we were in the middle of the sea).

Later, when the Spaniards returned after the Pueblo Revolt of 1680, families began to establish rancherias east of the earlier Spanish settlements, including the Llano Estacado. A hardy breed of Spanish cattle referred to as Longhorns proliferated

Left: A '68 Pontiac Bonneville rests beside a former gas station and Valentine-style diner in Glenrio.

in the harsh, waterless Llano grasslands.

After the War with Mexico, American ranchers moved into this same region. In the 1850s, men like John Chisum, Charles Goodnight, Oliver Loving, and Lucien Maxwell bought up Spanish land-grant rancherias or established their own. In the early 1860s, things got out of hand as the country became engaged in the Civil War and Texas seceded and became a part of the Confederacy. Various Indian tribes, such as the Kiowas, Comanches, and Apaches, took advantage and launched attacks on isolated ranches. After a bitter campaign against the Navajos and Mescalero Apaches, these two tribes were rounded up and relocated to a reservation at Fort Sumner (see Side Trip, page 22).

To provide military protection to these ranches, as well as travelers and traders, the Military Commander of New Mexico, General James H. Carleton authorized the construction of Fort Bascom on the Canadian River opposite the mouth of Ute Creek. The fort was named in honor of Captain George Bascom, who was killed on February 21, 1862, at the Battle of Valverde. One of the fort's first major campaigns was led by Colonel Christopher (Kit) Carson in 1864. Following the Canadian River through the Texas panhandle, they came upon a major Kiowa village and chased the inhabitants away. Continuing on the march along the Canadian River, the troopers, accompanied by two mountain howitzers, were now being confronted by more and more mounted Kiowa and Comanche warriors. When they came to William Bent's old trading post, now just ruined adobe walls, the soldiers set up a barricaded encampment. Throughout the day, November 25, they were attacked by about 1,000 mounted warriors, who repeatedly charged from different points and were consistently repulsed. The engagement is now known as the First Battle of Adobe Walls.

Fort Bascom led a fairly active military life until December 1870, when the garrison was transferred to Fort Union. Five miles west, a town provided the soldiers with a saloon and other entertainment. The soldiers called it "Liberty" because it was the one place where they were under no restraints.

After Fort Bascom was abandoned, Liberty lived on as a small ranching community until the turn of the century when the railroad pushed through eight miles to the south. Realizing the railroad's significance, the citizens packed up their goods, dismantled some buildings, and moved the town south to form the nucleus of Tucumcari, New Mexico.

Meanwhile, one of the most colorful characters of nineteenth-century New Mexico decided to settle down in the villa de Taos in 1841, when it was still a part of the Republic of Mexico. Lucien Bonaparte Maxwell was born in southern Illinois in 1818. At 23, he had already been a trapper, mountain man, hunter, army scout, Indian fighter, and Indian trader. Over the next thirty-four years he also became an Indian agent, farmer, rancher, sheepman, stockbreeder, miner, land baron, millionaire, bank president, judge, and friend of Kit Carson. He and his wife Luz Beaubien, had six children.

By the American Civil War, Maxwell had expanded his land holdings throughout northeast New Mexico and into southern Colorado. By 1870, his holdings amounted to 1,714,764 acres.

John Chisum (portrayed by John Wayne in the 1970 movie, *Chisum*) was one of the largest individual cattle owners in the United States and left an indelible mark on the history of west Texas and east-central New Mexico. During the Civil War, he raised cattle in southwestern Texas, but in 1866 relocated to eastern New Mexico. For the next fifteen years, his cattle watered on the Pecos River and grazed along the western slope of the Llano Estacado.

Two other west Texas cattlemen, Charles Goodnight and Oliver Loving, began moving cattle up the Rio Pecos valley to Fort Sumner in 1866, over what is now known as the Goodnight-Loving Trail. During this time, Goodnight invented the chuck wagon when he rebuilt an army surplus ambulance wagon for more practical use as a mobile unit for the camp's cook.

This mixture of cattle barons, unscrupulous merchants, combative Indians, mentally fatigued Civil War veterans, gamblers, cattle rustlers, frus-

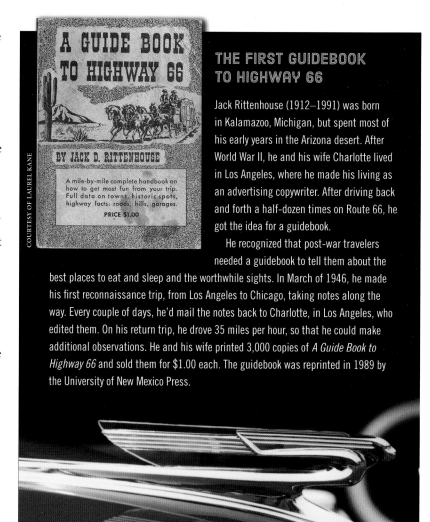

THE FIRST GUIDEBOOK TO HIGHWAY 66

Jack Rittenhouse (1912–1991) was born in Kalamazoo, Michigan, but spent most of his early years in the Arizona desert. After World War II, he and his wife Charlotte lived in Los Angeles, where he made his living as an advertising copywriter. After driving back and forth a half-dozen times on Route 66, he got the idea for a guidebook.

He recognized that post-war travelers needed a guidebook to tell them about the best places to eat and sleep and the worthwhile sights. In March of 1946, he made his first reconnaissance trip, from Los Angeles to Chicago, taking notes along the way. Every couple of days, he'd mail the notes back to Charlotte, in Los Angeles, who edited them. On his return trip, he drove 35 miles per hour, so that he could make additional observations. He and his wife printed 3,000 copies of *A Guide Book to Highway 66* and sold them for $1.00 each. The guidebook was reprinted in 1989 by the University of New Mexico Press.

trated gold miners, and homesteaders was bound to erupt in a bloody mess. The Lincoln County War of 1878–1880 fit that recipe.

By 1880, telegraph lines were installed throughout the region, and the railroads were expanding their lines. There was no longer a need to drive cattle north into Colorado or Kansas to reach stockyards at Abilene, Topeka, or Fort Lyon. Now, the Kansas Pacific Railroad had extended a line south to Tulsa and then continued into northern Texas. The Atchison, Topeka and Santa Fe Railway, taking a more northern route, was already steaming into Albuquerque.

In the late 1890s, another railroad, the Chicago, Rock Island and Pacific established a terminal about eight miles south of Liberty. Those town folk recognized the railroad's importance and wasted no time relocating their community adjacent to the tracks. Initially, it was a railroad worker tent city known as Six Shooter Siding, but by 1901 it became known as Tucumcari, from the Comanche term tukamukaru (to lie in wait for someone). The high mesa called tukamukaru to the south of the town was used as a lookout for Comanche war parties.

By the first decade of the twentieth century, the buffalo were gone, and wagons and buggies were scarcely seen anymore. Crossing this endless sea of grass were early models of automobiles and trucks, whose drivers were adding their voices to the growing demand for a better grade of road.

In 1913, William H. "Coin" Harvey, assisted by Cy Avery of Tulsa, organized the Ozark Trails Association. These farsighted businessmen developed a network of locally maintained roads that predated the U.S. federal highway system. The roads ran from St. Louis to Tulsa and Oklahoma City, and then branched out to El Paso, Texas, and Las Vegas, New Mexico.

One of these roads connected Oklahoma City to Amarillo, Texas, and then went on to Tucumcari, Santa Rosa, and Las Vegas, New Mexico. Along all the Ozark Trails, cement obelisks were erected high enough to be seen over the carpet of grasses, with "O.T." painted in green with the distance to the next town. Four are still in place between the New Mexico state line and Tucumcari.

Small town wagon yards and blacksmith shops were being replaced by filling stations and cafés. One such town, Glenrio, was mostly built on the Texas side of the border, but later expanded into New Mexico. A railroad depot was established here in 1906 and by 1926, when long segments of the Ozark Trail became incorporated into the newly

designated U.S. Route 66, Glenrio was already a tourist center. Around 1930, Route 66 between Glenrio and San Jon was realigned a mile to the north, with four creosote-treated timber bridges built in 1930 and rebuilt in 1947. In 1936 this was the first segment to be paved.

The major tourist facility in Glenrio was the Texas Longhorn Motel & Café. A large sign alerted westbound travelers that this is the "Last Stop in Texas," while on the other side it was the "First Stop in Texas." The Texas side was a dry county (no alcoholic sales), so customers at the café or motel walked across the state line into New Mexico to the State Line Bar and Gas Station, which sold candy, cigarettes, groceries, cold pop, and a full assortment of beer, wine, and whiskey.

Today, the only site still carrying the Glenrio name is Russell's Truck & Travel Center of Glenrio, about a half-mile to the north on I-40, at Exit 369. The large facility has an impressive display of thirty restored classic cars, gas pumps, neon signs, and a nostalgia-themed 66 Diner. A car show is held there every Memorial Day weekend. They even remind you to change your watches from Central Standard Time (Texas) to Mountain Standard Time (New Mexico).

About four miles west was the small hamlet of Endee, named for the N-D Ranch, on whose land it was situated. It maintained the oldest post office in the area, established in 1886 until the town closed in 1955.

Motorcyclists on the Mother Road near the New Mexico/Texas border.

Left: Elvis Presley, Betty Boop, and Marilyn Monroe celebrate the era of Route 66 inside Russell's Truck & Travel Center in Glenrio.

Right: Collectibles and a pink '57 Ford Thunderbird in the Car and Collectible Museum inside Russell's Truck & Travel Center.

The next spot down the line was Bard, named for the local Bar-D Ranch. This site moved every time Route 66 was realigned, and suffered the same fate as Endee.

San Jon (pronounced San Hone) is the next settlement going west. Like Budville, it took advantage of a federal statute that gave towns the right to object to any construction of federal highways that would adversely affect their local economy. The proposed route of the new interstate bypassed them by almost five miles.

Consequently, throughout the late 1960s, construction of the forty-mile segment of I-40 between Tucumcari and Glenrio was delayed while the dispute between San Jon and the Federal Highway Commission was settled. Meanwhile, traffic had to be diverted to the old Route 66. That section became known as "Slaughter Lane" because of the numerous injuries and fatal traffic accidents, stemming from tremendous amounts of traffic for a two-lane highway and rough, narrow paving. Finally, in November 1969, federal and state officials agreed to alter the proposed route, bringing the interstate bypass up to the town's northern limits. In 1981 the completed forty-mile stretch was finally open to the public. Oddly, this section of Route 66 was the first to be paved in 1936, and the same stretch of I-40 was the last segment in New Mexico to be paved, completed in 1981.

From San Jon into Tucumcari, the paved section of the 1950s alignment of Route 66 pretty well parallels the present I-40. You can spot a few cement bridges identified by metal disks as 1936 Works Progress Administration projects. If you follow Route 66 to I-40 at Exit 335, continue until you intersect Tucumcari Boulevard/Historic Route 66, then turn left, and enjoy the town!

Tucumcari was made famous by all of its billboards—"Tucumcari Tonite!"—three hundred miles in either direction along Route 66 and I-40. Along the five-mile stretch through the heart of Tucumcari, one is constantly reminded of the Route 66 glory days.

Blue Swallow
MOTEL
100% REFRIGERATED AIR
VACANCY
TV
LOBBY
Genuine
OPEN
HISTORIC PROPERTY
+
INSPECTION INVITED
+
TRUCK & RV PARKING

The LEGENDARY ROAD

Above: A giant Tucumcari Route 66 mural by Doug and Sharon Quarles.

Right: The Spanish Mission-style train depot first opened in the late 1920s and now houses a train museum. The Tucumcari depot once served the Rock Island-Southern Pacific lines.

Left: As dusk falls, the Blue Swallow Motel neon shines brightly above the '51 Pontiac waiting out front.

The most noted landmark is the Blue Swallow Motel, built in 1939, completely refurbished, and still accommodating Route 66 "roadies." Across the street is the equally well-known Motel Safari, built in 1959, and owned and operated by Richard and Gail Talley. Richard is a walking encyclopedia of local Route 66 history, and was partially responsible for the New Mexico Route 66 Museum. This museum is located in the Tucumcari Convention Center and includes the fantastic exhibit of 166 photos by Michael Campanelli from the Route 66 Photo Museum. The main museum displays the "Route 66 Memorial," probably the world's largest mural devoted to Route 66, a number of vintage cars and trucks, and Route 66 memorabilia from Glenrio to Gallup.

Only a block away is Tee Pee Curios, which began in 1944 and today is one of the last curio stores on Route 66 between Amarillo and Albuquerque.

The recently restored Spanish Mission-style train depot, built in the 1920s, stands a couple of blocks

Marilyn Monroe graces the New Mexico Route 66 Museum.

Below right: A Route 66 Monument marks the Tucumcari Convention Center with a gigantic chrome fin and tail lights that glow at night.

Overleaf: Taking a spin on the popular carnival rides at the Quay County Fair held in August.

north on Main Street. For many years, the restaurant across the street was "Harry's Lunch." The colorful owner, Harry Garrison, wearing a showy Western outfit and a pair of pearl-handled pistols, would greet each passenger train. In 1948, after pop singer Dorothy Shay was among the passengers welcomed by Garrison, she wrote the popular song, "Two-Gun Harry from Tucumcari."

A Dempster windmill built with wood blades catches sunrise at the Tucumcari Historical Museum.

Below: All the bronze skeletons in Mesalands Community College's Dinosaur Museum and Natural Sciences Laboratory, like this forty-foot-long Torvosaurus, were cast in the College's foundry.

Right: The Tee Pee Curios neon lights up Route 66 like its done since the 1960s. Tee Pee Curios opened as a Gulf gas station, grocery store, and souvenir shop in 1944. The neon sign was restored in 2003.

The Tucumcari Historical Museum, located in a 1904 schoolhouse, displays many items representing the various cultures of Quay County. Nearby on the corner of 1st and Laughlin Streets is Mesalands Community College's Dinosaur Museum, which hosts the largest collection of life-size bronze dinosaur skeletons in the world.

Most travelers use Exit 331 to leave Tucumcari and continue west, but the old Route 66 can be negotiated for another two miles to Exit 329. At this point, however, it is best to get on the interstate because the remnants of Route 66 are not maintained. A couple of miles farther west, the 1936 cement bridge crosses Blanco Wash, just east of Palomas Mesa. For the next ten miles a paved segment of Route 66 passes through Parajito Creek Valley, serving as a frontage road for local farmers and residents. Montoya was once a busy town and a major cattle-shipping point, but all that's left are some vacant buildings, including Richardson's Store, which was the last business to remain on Route 66 there.

West of Montoya an old New Mexico Historical Marker tells the story of the Goodnight Cattle Trail, blazed in 1866. Between 1959 and 1965, several episodes of the CBS TV program *Rawhide*, starring Clint Eastwood and Eric Fleming, were filmed in this area.

The twenty-mile stretch between Montoya and Cuervo generally follows the earlier Ozark Trail alignment. Newkirk is basically a ghost town serving as the junction of Highway 129 that goes north seventeen miles to Mesa Rica, and then another five miles, as Highway 432, to Conchas Lake State Park.

Another nine miles brings you to Cuervo, a predominately Hispanic village. From here into Santa Rosa, about eighteen miles distant, there are two choices if you want to continue driving on Route 66. The 1932 alignment goes south for seven miles and then due west, where it becomes part of Highway 156 as it proceeds into Santa Rosa. The first seven miles are not maintained and can be rough going at times. The other option is the 1952 alignment, which is close to the present interstate and still serves as a local road.

As you approach the eastern outskirts of Santa Rosa, look for the intersection with Highway 84. Take this road south to Fort Sumner for an interesting Side Trip.

FORT SUMNER

From Santa Rosa, go thirty-two miles south to the town of Fort Sumner on Highway 84. Founded in 1906, it was originally called Sunnyside, and consisted of seven saloons, three restaurants, and a lot of tents. After the railroad built its bridge across the Pecos River, the town continued to grow but under the name of Fort Sumner. The railroad still functions as part of the Burlington Northern and Santa Fe system.

Visit the Billy the Kid Museum. Established in 1953 by Ed Sweet, the museum is much more than a memorial to a 21-year-old renegade named William Bonney. Among the 60,000 relics on view are antique cars, wagons and buggies, saddles and horse equipment, almost every type of gun ever used in the Southwest, and personal belongings of General Edwin Vose Sumner (for whom the fort was named). They also have the rifle that may have once belonged to Billy the Kid and a rock on which he had carved his name. Fort Sumner is about four miles south.

HISTORY OF THE FORT ➣—▸

In 1852 and again in 1854, Captain James H. Carleton and the First Dragoons explored and mapped the Pecos River valley. He felt the area had a great military and agricultural value. The local inhabitants called the area "Bosque Redondo" (round woods). Shortly afterward, Carleton was reassigned to a post in California.

In 1862, Carleton, now a brigadier general, returned to New Mexico as commander of the California Column, which marched to the area in response to the Texan Confederate invasion. At the end of October 1862, he ordered the establishment of a military post at the Bosque Redondo.

Carleton had also ordered five companies of New Mexico Volunteer Cavalry, under the command of Colonel Christopher (Kit) Carson, to reoccupy the abandoned Fort Stanton and to vigorously pursue a campaign against the Mescalero Apache. The campaign lasted until February 1863 and resulted in over five hundred Mescalero Apaches being brought in. Previously, Carleton had officially designated an area of forty miles square (about one million acres) adjacent to Fort Sumner, as the Bosque Redondo Reservation for these Mescalero Apaches.

Carleton's attention was then directed toward the Navajos, and he used the same military tactics he had successfully used against the Apaches.

In the summer of 1863, Kit Carson, with a number of mounted units, reoccupied the abandoned Fort Defiance (and renamed it Fort Canby, in honor of General E. R. S. Canby). Another fort, recently built at San Rafael, and named after Captain Benjamin Wingate, was also a part of the campaign against the Navajos.

Throughout the fall of 1863, military units from both forts ravaged the Navajo countryside, destroying the autumn harvest, killing livestock, burning hogans, and killing any Navajos who resisted this military onslaught.

During the winter of 1863–64, the surviving Navajos, impoverished, starving, and sick, began to surrender at Fort Canby and Fort Wingate. Before long, both posts were completely overwhelmed.

General Carleton then made a fateful decision—relocate the Navajos, as well, to the reservation at Bosque Redondo. But unlike marching five hundred Apaches ninety miles from Fort Stanton to Fort Sumner, the military was now confronted with relocating more than 6,000 Navajos on a grueling 350-mile march. The Navajo Long Walk had begun.

During the subsequent four years of captivity, the Navajos and Apaches tried to make a living by tilling the alkaline soil, and protecting their few small herds of horses and sheep from Comanche raids, while enduring harsh weather, drought, and infestations of corn worms and grasshoppers. The Apaches got fed up with the system, and on the night of November 3, 1865, left the Bosque Redondo. Before leaving, they stole two hundred Navajo horses.

In late May 1868, General William T. Sherman and Colonel Samuel Tappan visited the Bosque Redondo Reservation and were appalled at the wretched conditions. They initiated three days of intense negotiations with a dozen Navajo leaders, which resulted in a Treaty of Peace (which is still in effect today) that allowed the surviving 7,300 Navajos to return to their traditional homeland. In early 1869, the last military unit withdrew from Fort Sumner.

BILLY THE KID ➣—▸

Henry McCarty was born in New York City on November 23, 1859. His parents, William McCarty and Catherine Bonney, were poor Irish immigrants. He had one brother, Joe. When William died, Catherine took her two sons to Indiana. In 1873, she married William Antrim and they settled in Silver City, New Mexico. The following year, Catherine died of tuberculosis and Antrim left the two boys to fend for themselves.

In 1877, Henry was working in a sawmill at Camp Grant Army Post when he got into a fight with the blacksmith, Frank Cahill, and killed him. Henry fled to Mesilla, New Mexico, where he changed his name, taking the first name of his father and stepfather, William, and his mother's maiden name, Bonney.

WIKIMEDIA COMMONS

Billy the Kid.

He hired on as a ranch-hand for John Tunstall, just in time to become embroiled in the Lincoln County War. "The Kid" joined a posse known as the Regulators who fought on one side of the Lincoln County War, and took credit for killing Sheriff William Brady and several others.

The gang's luck ran out in December 1880, when a posse under the new sheriff, Pat Garrett, surprised and killed one of the Regulators, Tom O'Falliard. Three days later, Garrett's posse surrounded them and killed Charlie Bowdre. William "Billy" Bonney and the two survivors surrendered.

Bonney was convicted of Sheriff Brady's murder and sentenced to hang. But on April 28, 1881, Billy overpowered and killed the deputies guarding him and escaped the Lincoln County courthouse.

Sheriff Pat Garrett eventually traced Billy to Fort Sumner. Late in the evening of July 14, 1881, Garrett was in the darkened bedroom of Pete Maxwell, talking about the elusive Billy when a figure appeared in the doorway and asked, "Pete, is that you?" Garrett recognized the voice, fired two shots, and it was all over. The man in the doorway was, indeed, Billy the Kid—and now he passed into legend.

The Depression of 1893 took a heavy toll on the cattle industry. By 1900, many small communities, including old Fort Sumner, were abandoned. Eventually, the adobe walls melted back into the earth, or were ravaged by a couple of severe Pecos River floods. All that was left was a forlorn cemetery.

As a result of popular novels and films about Billy the Kid,

in 1932, a museum/gift shop was constructed adjacent to the cemetery, to both serve visitors and provide some protection to the graves. Now known as the Old Fort Sumner Museum, it contains a wealth of information and relics.

THE FORT TODAY ⊳→

In 1968, the Navajo Nation made arrangements to hold a centennial commemoration at the site, and the local people extended their full cooperation. The June 29–30 event was a reenactment of the Treaty of Peace signing, and was attended by hundreds, including many Navajo officials.

On June 4, 2005, state and local dignitaries joined several hundred members of the Mescalero Apache and Navajo tribes to dedicate a memorial to the Bosque Redondo at Fort Sumner State Monument. The facility includes excellent exhibits and dioramas, a research center, and a tour of some of the partially restored original fort buildings.

The town of Fort Sumner holds the annual Old Fort Days on the second weekend in June. The event features a parade, arts and crafts fair, and the Billy the Kid Tombstone Race, in which participants carry a replica of his original grave marker in a 100-yard race.

Billy the Kid's grave at Fort Sumner.

CHAPTER 3

RETRIBUTION ROAD

SANTA ROSA TO MORIARTY TO TIJERAS CANYON

SANTA ROSA, sixty miles west of Tucumcari, began as a ranching area in 1824 when Don Antonio Sandoval was given a land grant by the Republic of Mexico. In 1865, Don Celso Baca, an officer in Colonel Kit Carson's First Regiment of New Mexico Volunteers during the Navajo Campaign, began ranching on El Rito Creek east of the Pecos River. Baca developed a cattle empire that lasted until 1910. His headquarters, known as the Don Celso Territorial House, has been restored. He built a private chapel across the entrance road and dedicated it to Saint Rose of Lima (Santa Rosa).

A post office using the name Santa Rosa opened in 1873 on the west bank of the Pecos River. It closed in 1898, but the community of Eden across the river changed its name to Santa Rosa.

In late 1901, when the railhead of the Chicago, Rock Island and Pacific reached the Pecos River, the construction crews amounted to almost four thousand workers. A proliferation of saloons, cafés, and gambling houses appeared, but as the crews moved farther west, the community settled back into ranching and farming, until Route 66 began to bring tourists in the 1930s.

The first attempt at a road through Santa Rosa was the Ozark Trail, which came west from Texas, through Tucumcari, and then into Santa Rosa. As Route 66 was being established in 1926, it followed the Ozark Trail, through Santa Rosa, and then northward to Romero-

ville, a few miles short of Las Vegas.

The most notable attraction then was the Blue Hole, an artesian spring, ninety feet deep and sixty feet wide, coming out of a bell-shaped cleft in the local granite formation. The clean and clear water, at a constant 64°F, flows at 3,000 gallons per minute and is highly alkaline, causing an aquamarine color. Today, the Blue Hole is still a popular destination for swimmers and scuba divers. Nearby, you can still see the two faded 66-era "billboards" painted on boulders.

From 1926 until 1937, Route 66 ran past the Blue Hole, but then was realigned more to the north, through the center of town (now known as Will Rogers Drive/Parker Avenue). During its heyday, there were over sixty gas stations, twenty motels, and fifteen restaurants in Santa Rosa, including the Club Café, built in 1935. When Philip Craig and Ron Shaw took over in 1935, they introduced the logo that made the café popular—a smiling Fat Man, which was emblazoned on billboards all along Route 66. The Club Café building was demolished in 2005, but the

Left: Songs like "Wake Up Little Susie" and "Whole Lotta Shakin' Goin' On" rock the jukebox at Joseph's Bar and Grill in Santa Rosa.

Top right: The Blue Hole is a popular swimming destination.

Right: The smiling man who once adorned the Club Café has been rescued by James "Bozo" Cordova and is displayed inside his Route 66 Auto Museum in Santa Rosa.

Fat Man lives on at Joseph's Restaurant a half-block away. La Mesa Motel and the La Loma Lodge, operating since the 1950s, are still open.

Visitors to the "City of Natural Lakes" can enjoy swimming, boating, fishing, and camping at Santa Rosa Lake State Park, north of town. The lake was created when a dam was built on the Pecos River in 1954. Park Lake, just west of Blue Hole, is surrounded by a playground and offers fun and swimming opportunities for the entire family. Perch Lake on Highway 91 south of town also offers water-related activities.

Check out the Route 66 Auto Museum, off I-40 at Exit 277. The museum is on the south side of the road and offers exhibits on Route 66 memorabilia and over thirty vehicles—an awesome assortment of classics, vintage cars and trucks, and even flame-kissed street rods. And many of the cars are for sale! You can also track down a local car show through their connection with the New Mexico Council of Car Clubs.

Going west out of Santa Rosa you gradually climb out of the Pecos River valley. Seven miles out of town Exit 267 connects you to County Road 4H, and it was here in 1926 that Governor Arthur Hannett's "get-even" road started.

The Interstate overlays or is adjacent to the original Route 66 as it takes you to Moriarty, seventy-six miles to the west. It cuts arrow straight through several piñon and juniper forests, with the occa-

sional ranch house. This country may seem barren, but it is steeped in the wonderful literary heritage of Rudolfo Anaya, author of *Bless Me, Ultima* and several other stories, novels, and plays from the local culture.

The pre-1937 route north to Santa Fe begins at Exit 256, where Highway 84 North takes you to Dilia and Apache Springs before connecting with I-25 at Romeroville. But that's another adventure (see Side Trip to Santa Fe).

MURALS ALONG ROUTE 66

Public art appears in almost every New Mexico town along old Route 66, reflecting individual and community pride. Three small towns in particular—Tucumcari, Moriarty, and Gallup—are good examples of developing and preserving murals.

In Tucumcari, Doug Quarles created about two-dozen outdoor murals between 2003 and 2008, sometimes with the help of his wife, Sharon, while operating a combined studio, gallery, and bed-and-breakfast. The murals became quite popular as residents realized that they not only reflected historic events but were also tourist attractions.

Other artists joined in, and soon there were murals at Conchas Dam, Logan High School, San Jon High School, and the Tucumcari Convention Center. Some of the more unique subjects include, "Ranch Scene," "Tucumcari Lumber," "66 Eyes on Route 66," "The Legendary Road," and "Where's My Horse?" Still one of the biggest attractions, though, is Doug and Sharon's joint composition of the world's largest mural devoted to Route 66 in this country. It takes up a whole wall in the New Mexico Route 66 Museum.

Another small town that has brightened up its main-street area is Moriarty. With encouragement from RETRO and New Mexico MainStreet, four businesses and the Chamber of Commerce offered outdoor wall space. By 2014, five murals had been completed by local artists: "The Mother Road" by Tony Jaramillo Jr., "Mike's Friendly Store" by Elizabeth Harris, "Retribution Road" by Paul Harmon, "Lisa's Truck Center" by Willy Fisher, and "Get Your Kicks on Route 66" by Robin Matlack.

Finally, Gallup has been a source of public murals going back to Works Project Administration times. Two murals in the McKinley County Courthouse were painted in 1939. More recently, artist Be Sargent created a large mural on 2nd Street to honor the Navajo Code Talkers of World War II. This mural received such wide acclaim that Sargent was commissioned to do five more.

In 2004, eight more outdoor murals were financed, each with its own subject and artist. A year or so later, the downtown area was a much more colorful and entertaining place. Gallup City Hall has two murals—the "Great Gallup Mural" by Paul Newman and Steve Heil, and the "Gallup Community Life" montage by Ric Sarracino. The historical "Zuni" mural by Geddy Epaloose is on the Octavia Fellin Public Library. On a Coal Avenue building, Navajo artist Irving Bahe painted scenes from the "Gallup Inter-Tribal Indian Ceremonial." Across the street is a vivid mural of the "Coal Mining Era," in which artist Andrew Butler used only the three primary colors. A block away on Aztec Avenue, Erica Rae Sykes's modern approach recognizes "Women's Multi-Cultural Mural" involvement in the history of Gallup. And a mural by Richard Yazzie portrays the "Long Walk Home" of the Navajo people in 1868.

Probably the most prolific painter of the bunch was Chester Kahn. His large, detailed mural, "Native American Trading" is on the west wall of Tanner's Indian Arts on 3rd Street. He also painted a mural around the entire inside of the Ellis Tanner Trading Post just southwest of Gallup on Highway 602. This project, known as the "Circle of Light," includes more than sixty images of famous Native American men and women, and scenes depicting the Navajo Long Walk, the Code Talkers, and rodeos.

Ric Sarracino has added two more public murals to the downtown area recently. One, on east Coal Avenue, deals with the Hispanic involvement in Gallup area history, and the other, on the wall of Camille's restaurant on south 2nd Street, was done in a Japanese style and honors Medal of Honor recipient Hiroshi Miyamura.

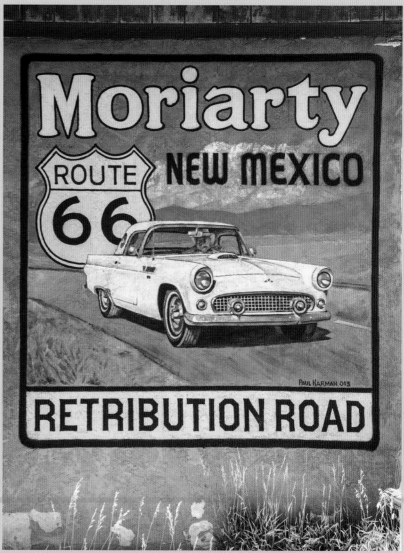

Top: This Gallup mural by Be Sargent honors the World War II Navajo Code Talkers.
Above: Paul Harmon's "Retribution Road" mural.
Right: Chester Kahn's 2005 "Native American Trading" mural in Gallup.

Continuing west, in twenty-two miles you arrive at Bowlin's Flying C Ranch and Travel Center. Built by Roy Cline in 1945, he operated a gas station, garage, and café. In 1963, he sold it to Bowlin Travel Centers, Inc., a family business that has grown greatly since Claude Bowlin started trading with the Navajos in 1912.

Another sixteen miles brings you to Clines Corners (Exit 218). In 1934, Roy Cline built a small restaurant, gas station, and souvenir shop at the junction of Route 66 and Highway 285. Although the facilities were rather small, Roy made up for it with a large sign and numerous billboards. He sold the place in 1939, and built the Flying C Ranch after World War II.

About fifteen miles farther west was one of the most popular attractions ever along Route 66. After driving for hours across eastern New Mexico, the Longhorn Ranch, constructed in the "Old West" style so popular in the movies, was a welcome sight, especially if you had kids in the car.

Bill Ehret, a former police captain, opened the trading post, gas station, and café in December 1940. After the war, he added a motel, restaurants, garage, curio shop, cocktail lounge, and a stage station where kids could take a ride in a horse-drawn Concord stagecoach. The Longhorn Ranch closed in 1977, and only the motel and lounge remain standing. Moriarty awaits seven miles away.

Moriarty was established in the 1890s as a small ranching community. Michael Moriarty came here from Iowa, looking for a warmer, drier climate for relief from his chronic arthritis. When the railroad was built and a post office was established in 1902, the town was named after him.

Central Avenue follows the earlier Route 66. A number of Moriarty businesses along here keep the spirit of Route 66 alive. A lot of credit goes to RETRO (RElive The ROute), a local Route 66 promotional group of volunteers. They work in cooperation with New Mexico MainStreet and the

Left: They say that Clines Corners is on your way to everywhere.

Below: The Moriarty Whiting Brothers service station sign was restored in 2014.

The Southwest Soaring Museum in Moriarty displays more than forty gliders and models covering New Mexico's history of soaring.

five recently painted Route 66 murals in town.

As you proceed to the west end of town, jog to the left and access Highway 333, which is the 1937 Route 66 for the next twenty-seven miles. Small ranches and farms, some still growing wheat or their ever-popular pinto beans, are scattered over the land, even up to the slopes of the Sandia and Manzano mountains.

In Edgewood don't miss the Wildlife West Nature Park. Roger Alink founded the non-profit organization dedicated to educating kids and adults on native wildlife and ecology. Here you will see owls, hawks, wolves, elk, javelina, pronghorn, and many more non-releasable rescue animals. The park also offers summertime chuck wagon suppers, hay rides, music festivals, and has an authentic Red Top Valentine diner.

After you pass Edgewood, you come to Sedillo. Sedillo Hill used to be Cherry Hill, where a well-advertised cherry cider stand used to offer a cool, delicious drink, especially nice if you were driving east out to the Llano. From here you begin to get into the canyon that encompasses the sprawling community of Tijeras.

As you approach the canyon's edge, you can get an awesome view of Albuquerque and the Rio Grande valley spread out before you. It'll be a 2,000-foot drop in elevation before you reach the Rio Grande. As Highway 333 turns into Central Avenue, this chapter comes to a close.

National Park Service Route 66 Corridor Preservation Program.

RETRO assisted in the restoration of the two signs at the Whiting Brothers service station owned by Sal Lucero, and held a lighting ceremony in December of 2014. During the heyday of Route 66, the Whiting Brothers had over one hundred stations. Now, the only one left is in Moriarty, New Mexico.

In Moriarty you will find fascinating collections at the Southwest Soaring (glider) Museum, the Lewis Antique Auto and Toy Museum, and the Moriarty Historical Society and Museum. Get Your Kicks Restaurant and Curio Store has one of the

Right: Cowboy gift shop sign at the Edgewood Wildlife West Nature Park and Rescued Wildlife Zoo.

Far right: Flicker the pronghorn antelope is the offspring of Princess Vela, both rescued animals at the Wildlife West Nature Park.

Side Trip

THE SANTA FE LOOP

This side trip follows the early route of the Ozark Trail, the Santa Fe Trail, and the even earlier Camino Real de Tierra Adentro, as Route 66 eventually overlaid these historic trails. We will take the current Highway 84 North, at I-40 Exit 256.

This road will take you north sixteen miles to the small settlement of Dilia, which consists of some old adobe dwellings, homes, and the well-maintained Sacred Heart Catholic Church.

Travelling north from Dilia, you approach the Pecos Wilderness and drive through Apache Springs and Los Montoyas. The junction of Highway 84 with I-25 is located in what is left of Romeroville, home to a number of former cafés, gas stations, and lodgings. At this junction, it is a five-mile trip east on I-25 to the historic community of Las Vegas.

In 1835, twenty-nine individuals received the Las Vegas Land Grant from the Mexican government. In true Spanish fashion, the settlers laid out a plaza as the nucleus for the proposed village of Las Vegas, or "The Meadows." Situated on the Santa Fe Trail, the town became a supply and mercantile center. In 1880, the AT&SF railway arrived at the town, and Las Vegas's population and wealth grew. Today, the community prides itself on having roughly nine hundred structures on the National Register of Historic Places. Las Vegas is also home to the 50,000-square-foot Mission Revival–style Castañeda Hotel. A Fred Harvey hotel

Downtown Las Vegas, New Mexico.

opened in 1898, it was the first of three luxurious stops on the Santa Fe line, along with the Alvarado in Albuquerque and El Tovar at Grand Canyon's south rim. The hotel closed in 1948, but the owners of Arizona's La Posada hotel purchased it and began restoration in 2014.

Some of the original 1926–1937 route of Highway 66 can still be found behind rangeland fences or disguised as access roads throughout this corridor. This is the same pathway established by the William Becknell party that laid out the initial Santa Fe Trail route in 1821 between St. Louis, Missouri, and Santa Fe. The railroad brought about the Santa Fe Trail's demise. Ironically, the Santa Fe Railway never actually entered Santa Fe. The closest it got was the passenger station at Lamy, twelve miles south of the capital city.

In 1926, some intersecting roads between Santa Rosa and Santa Fe were connected with the designation of Route 66. For the next decade, this section was constantly realigned. In 1937, when it was declassified as Route 66, it was designated as Highways 85 and 84. During the following years, realignments of both highways disrupted the continuity of old Route 66, and still later, the construction of I-25 buried and obliterated more segments of both Route 66 and its sidekick highways, 84 and 85. This leaves today's Route 66 aficionados facing a complicated collection of tangled fragments scattered from one end of this Side Trip to the other.

A short distance west of Romeroville is the settlement of Tecolote, with a combination of Pueblo and Hispanic occupants. From here to Bernal, parts of pre-1937 Route 66 can be seen but are not accessible. At San Jose del Vado you will cross the Pecos River (again).

When you get to Rowe, Exit 307, turn right onto Highway 63. This short excursion covers some of the most historic sites in the entire Southwest. Your first stop is the Kozlowski Ranch and Stage Station. The stage station also served as Camp Lewis, the Federal base camp during the Civil War Battle of Glorieta Pass.

Less than a mile down the road is the entrance to Pecos National Historic Park. Take the walking, self-guided tour through the major ancient pueblo of Pecos. This was a large and prosperous pueblo when visited by Don Juan de Oñate's colonizing army in 1598. Over the decades, this pueblo was subjected to harsh Spanish colonial practices and religious policies. In August 1680, the inhabitants participated in the Pueblo Revolt. By the early 1700s, Pecos was back as a partner with Spanish civil and religious authorities, but their importance as a trading center had diminished. The last occupants left the village in 1838 and moved in with their Towa-speaking relatives at Jemez Pueblo. Both the pueblo and the mission have been a part of the National Park Service since 1965.

Another good tour at Pecos is a two-mile hiking trail along a well-marked pathway in one of two nearby 300-acre tracts that preserve the sites of the 1862 Civil War Battle of Glorieta Pass. Visitors must make arrangements with the Pecos Park Rangers

This underground kiva at Pecos National Historical Park was an important structure for religious and ceremonial purposes.
Below left: El Santuario de Chimayo. **Below right:** The La Fonda Hotel was a Fred Harvey property.

prior to driving to the Battlefield parking lot and trailhead.

Another option is to drive north on Highway 63 to the small town of Pecos. Take a left turn onto Highway 50 and go about four miles to the historical marker at Pigeon's Ranch. There you will find the last remaining building—a field hospital for Federal troops—that played an important role in the Battle of Glorieta Pass.

Continue west on Highway 50 until it dead-ends at Exit 299 and then access I-25 for a short drive into Glorieta. At Glorieta, old Route 66 reemerges as the north-side frontage road Highway 84/85, and connects with Highway 285. In the next fifteen miles it becomes the Old Pecos Trail, the Old Santa Fe Trail, and finally Water Street in downtown Santa Fe.

Santa Fe is the oldest state capital in the United States. And it was also the oldest city on Route 66 between 1926 and 1937, when Route 66 went through the town. In 2010, Santa Fe celebrated its 400th birthday.

Between 1610 and 1612, the Spanish colonists moved from their 1598 settlement of San Gabriel del Yunque to this better-situated community, which Governor Pedro de Peralta officially recognized as the Royal Town of the Holy Faith of St. Francis de Assisi (La Villa Real de la Santa Fe de San Francisco de Asís).

One of the more famous buildings, dating back to 1612, is the Palace of the Governors. In 1821, the Republic of Mexico gained its independence. Twenty-five years later, the Army of the West entered Santa Fe in August 1846, and General Stephen W. Kearney declared that the Provincia de Nuevo Mejico was part of the United States of America.

During the time Route 66 bisected the downtown area between 1926 and 1937, there were only two major hotels in town, the La Fonda and the Hotel St. Francis. La Fonda, built in 1922, was purchased two years later by the Fred Harvey Company. The company brought in architect John Gaw Meem and interior designer Mary Elizabeth Jane Colter and by 1929 had doubled the hotel's size.

The Hotel St. Francis sits one block west of La Fonda. Originally known as the De Vargas Hotel, it was the favorite lodging of state politicians when the legislature was in session at the state capitol two blocks away.

Around the corner is the newer Inn and Spa at Loretto, which is built in the same Pueblo-Spanish style. Adjacent to the inn is the historic Loretto Chapel and its famous mystery staircase. When the Sisters of Loretto had a chapel built in 1878, the architect forgot to design a stairway up to the choir loft, and

CONTINUED ➤

Cathedral Basilica of St. Francis of Assisi.

Another summer-long event is the internationally recognized Santa Fe Opera. This unique facility, located seven miles north of Santa Fe, is a semi-outdoor theater known for introducing new operas as well as presentations of traditional European operas.

And don't forget the food! Dining in Santa Fe can also be an experience to remember. Many restaurants boast some of the finest culinary talent in the country, with menus

Hopi Kachina dolls line the wall at Bahti Indian Arts.

ranging from northern New Mexican chile dishes to European or continental cuisine.

To exit Santa Fe on a road that used to be Route 66, take Cerrillos Road south as it turns into Highway 85. You will see a number of old diners and restaurants, motels, grocery stores, and shops from the pre-1937 era that still exist along this route.

the nuns didn't like his proposed solution of a 22-foot ladder. The nuns prayed for guidance for nine days, when an itinerant worker with a toolbox appeared and asked about work. For weeks he quietly labored on the staircase, which, when finished, contained two complete spirals and a railing for both sides. No nails were used, just wooden pegs, and there was no visible means of support. While the nuns were preparing a farewell dinner of gratitude for him, the carpenter disappeared. No one in Santa Fe ever saw him again, or even knew his name.

Inn and Spa at Loretto.

Santa Fe is a city of museums; there are thirty-six in the area. A good one to start with is the New Mexico History Museum. It opened in 2009 and is connected to the Palace of the Governors, now also a museum. The Museum of Fine Art is a block west of the Palace of the Governors and includes collections of paintings by Taos and Santa Fe artists. The nearby Georgia O'Keeffe Museum is dedicated to her life and legacy.

South on Old Santa Fe Trail and right on Camino Lejo, there are four museums within walking distance: The Museum of New Mexico, Museum of International Folk Art, Museum of Indian Arts and Culture, and the Museum of Spanish Colonial Art. The Wheelwright Museum of the American Indian is down the street.

The Santa Fe Plaza is famous for its craft shops and galleries, as well as Pueblo Indian displays under the Palace of the Governors portal. Myriad outstanding shops and galleries specialize in Navajo rugs and blankets, Pueblo pottery, tribal baskets, Zuni fetishes, Hopi katsina carvings, a wide variety of silver and turquoise jewelry from several tribal traditions, and a prolific assortment of paintings.

The mysterious staircase in the Loretto Chapel.

At Exit 278, access I-25 for the trip down to Albuquerque.

Route 66 came to the lip of La Bajada, or "The Descent," about fifteen miles south of town. If you want to take a closer look at what's left of all these switchbacks, take Exit 264 and proceed west on Highway 16 for about three miles. You then come to an intersection with a paved road on the right that will take you to Tetilla Peak Recreation Area. From there you can see the hairpin turns on La Bajada Hill.

Continuing south along I-25 to Exit 259 (state road 22), you will reach the Santo Domingo Indian Trading Post. The original section of the post was built in 1880, but in 1922 a large, Mission-Revival-style building was added by the Seligman family. Starting in 1926, they claimed the complex as the oldest trading post on Route 66, and a large sign encouraged travelers to visit "The Most Interesting Spot in the Old West—Where Real Indians Trade." One of those visitors was President John F. Kennedy in 1962.

A few years ago, the Pueblo of Santo Domingo (also known by its original name, Kewa) purchased the site and both the 1880 structure and 1922 trading post have been restored and are now open for business.

The Santa Fe Plaza is the historic heart of Santa Fe where people continue to gather to this day.

Fire destroyed the 1922 Santo Domingo Trading Post in 2001, but it has been beautifully restored.

Two miles down the interstate, at Exit 257, you can get on old Route 66 and drive for about a quarter-mile south to the marker commemorating the Mormon Battalion.

Continuing south on the interstate, past the San Felipe Pueblo reservation, the old Route 66 is to the left. At the giant Tonque Arroyo wash (now the site of San Felipe's thriving roadside casino), the old highway climbed to a conspicuous, deep notch in the south ridge of the arroyo. Known as "The Big Cut," it is still visible from southbound I-25. When it was first constructed in 1909 as part of NM Route 1, it was boasted as a feat of modern engineering. Although only 18 feet wide and about 75 feet long, it was also used for Route 66 from 1926 to 1931, when the road was rerouted a half-mile to the west, where the interstate is now.

At Exit 242, take Highway 550 into the farming community of Bernalillo. Turn left onto Highway 313, and you will be on Route 66. Continue south past the Our Lady of Sorrows Church. Built in 1857, it combines features of Spanish/Mexican architecture with French elements brought to the area by the first Catholic bishop of New Mexico, Father Jean-Baptiste Lamy.

Heading south onto the Sandia Pueblo Reservation, Highway 313 becomes State Road 47, and then Fourth Street. The original alignment of NM Route 1, between Albuquerque and Alameda, is perhaps the first segment of rural highway to be paved in the entire state.

After about nine miles, Fourth Street nears downtown Albuquerque. Along a relatively quiet section of Fourth Street are a few businesses and the El Camino Motor Court that go back to the pre-1937 era of Route 66.

The City of Albuquerque expanded their downtown development and closed off Fourth Street at Marquette Street, just shy of Central Avenue. This forces the traveler to jog around a couple of blocks before getting back to the junction of Central and Fourth—the only place where Route 66, in its two alignments, essentially crossed itself.

A RIVER RUNS THROUGH IT

ALBUQUERQUE

ONCE YOU COME in sight of the rambling assortment of houses, businesses, and gas stations known as Tijeras Canyon, both I-40 and old Route 66 begin the long descent into the valley of the Rio Grande. The double canyon that separates the Sandia Mountains (north) from the Manzano Mountains (south) is shaped like a pair of scissors, or tijeras in Spanish. The roadway drops nearly 2,000 feet before it reaches the banks of the Great River (Rio Grande in Spanish) that runs through the largest city in New Mexico.

Prior to 1937, Route 66 officially ran through Santa Fe, which was the oldest city on the entire route, having been built in 1608. But after the realignment, Route 66 ran through Albuquerque, which could also claim the title "oldest city on Route 66," since it was established in 1706.

As the Spaniards regained control of the northern Rio Grande region after the Pueblo Revolt, the governor, Don Francisco Cuervo y Valdez, issued land grants to a dozen or so families along the Rio Grande. The April 23, 1706, proclamation created

COURTESY OF JOE SONDERMAN

a settlement named after the viceroy of New Spain, Don Francisco Fernandez de la Cueva Enriquez, eighth Duke of Alburquerque (thus, the nickname still in use today—Duke City). A public plaza was laid out, with a church on the north side and residences, government buildings, and merchant's stores on the other three sides.

In the winter of 1792, the original church collapsed during a blizzard, and the replacement was named after San Felipe de Neri, now the villa's patron.

For years the town served as a trade center for a largely agrarian society, and there wasn't much of an impact when the Mexican flag

Left: A shiny '47 Hudson Commodore Eight at the Enchanted Trails RV Park and Trading Post. The vintage '56 Yellowstone travel trailer has a luxurious hardwood birch interior.

Right: San Felipe de Neri Catholic Church in Old Town.

replaced the Spanish flag in 1821. However, in 1846, when the American flag replaced the Mexican flag, the changes were immediate and drastic.

The newcomers, mostly military at first, spoke a different language, had strange concepts of land ownership and governmental policies, and for the most part were non-Catholic. Then there was a short period of time when the U.S. flag was replaced by a Confederate banner. But the Civil War ended, initiating a steady flow of veterans, renegades, and homesteaders into New Mexico.

In the late 1870s, AT&SF Railway representatives scouted land near the villa plaza but found it too expensive. Instead, they made a secret deal with local businessmen to purchase cheaper land about a mile and a half east of town, and a station was constructed in the empty land at the foot of the Sandia Mountains.

On April 22, 1880, the first coal-burning steam engine pulled into the newly constructed railroad station. A band played fanfares, and speeches were delivered. And according to local legend, a new name was initiated, as the spelling of the town's name over the main entrance to the depot somehow left out one of the r's—Albuquerque. (It's more likely that the r was dropped over time due to Anglo mispronunciation.)

Laying tracks in an empty undeveloped area allowed a variety of business interests to establish themselves in a new economic center. Also, the once-profitable wagon freight industry that had bolstered the villa's economy during the preceding decade suddenly became obsolete. The future of Albuquerque would now belong to New Town, and the villa (now referred to as Old Town) would become increasingly irrelevant, although its cultural

influence would remain vital into the twenty-first century.

A road connecting Old Town and New Town was constructed and called Railroad Avenue. The gap between the two "towns" quickly filled with banks, mercantile stores, hotels, restaurants, and general businesses. Several health-care facilities and sanitariums for tuberculosis patients were built as Railroad Avenue extended east, and that section became known as "TB Row."

In 1889, with the founding of the University of New Mexico, the road was extended farther east to provide a connection with the railroad facilities. In 1907, the road became Central Avenue.

In the years following World War I, New Mexicans traded in their horses and wagons for automobiles and trucks. Even though it followed a rather circuitous path, the creation of Route 66 as a federal highway met with general approval. Fourth Street, the urban Route 66, became the nucleus for motor courts, campgrounds, cafés, garages, gas stations, and automobile dealerships.

After working to construct a road from Santa Rosa to Moriarty in 1926, State Highway Maintenance Superintendent Clyde Tingley lobbied for completion of the Santa Rosa cutoff. In 1930, he was appointed ex-officio mayor of Albuquerque and began to solicit federal New Deal funds to expand and realign Route 66.

Tingley had a bridge built over the Rio Grande in late 1931 at the west end of Central Avenue, allowing businesses and residences to expand on the west bank.

Above: The historic Bottger Mansion of Old Town, built in 1910, now houses a bed & breakfast.

Below: The Pueblo Revival-style Tewa Lodge opened in 1946.

COURTESY OF JOE SONDERMAN

The Tewa Lodge neon isn't original to the building, but it's a favorite along Route 66.

Avenue, and to the west the road over Nine-Mile Hill continued past the bridge on the Rio Puerco to Laguna Pueblo. Route 66, now using Central Avenue, became New Mexico's first completely oil-surfaced road, and the shortest east-west route.

Albuquerque's growing tourist industry responded quickly to the route change. By 1941, there were twenty-eight tourist camps on 4th Street and thirty-seven on Central Avenue. After World War II, when the population of Albuquerque was a little over 35,000, Central Avenue became the heart of the city's automobile life. By 1955, there were ninety-eight tourist courts and clusters of businesses that catered to the traveler—full-service gas stations, curio shops, drive-in restaurants, and Indian arts and crafts outlets. Fourth Street served the traffic flow from Santa Fe, but for some it was still considered to be a part of Route 66, so, for a while, the junction of 4th Street and Central Avenue became the only spot on the entire route where Route 66 intersected Route 66. Fourth Street south of Central Avenue had been the main thoroughfare leading to Los Lunas, until 1937 when that 56-mile stretch of Route 66 was replaced by the Laguna cutoff.

He then went on to become governor in 1934 and used his friendship with President Roosevelt to secure many New Deal projects, including the paving of many stretches of highway.

In 1936, Central Avenue climbed farther east out of the valley to service the Nob Hill area, the city's first shopping center, and the New Mexico State Fairgrounds, which had been reorganized that year.

By late 1937, the straightened east-west road, from Glenrio to Tijeras Canyon, was connected to Central

The 1950s marked both the heyday of Route 66 and the beginning of its demise. The route was widened on both the east and the west sides of the city, and in 1951 a second span was added across the Rio Grande. Old Town began to shift from a neighborhood center to a tourist attraction.

Albuquerque's 66 Diner, Kimberly Preston waitress.

As plans were made to replace Route 66 with a new interstate system, and shopping malls and chain franchises appeared, the city grew more to the north and east. The new metropolitan area on the west bank of the Rio Grande, Rio Rancho, has witnessed phenomenal growth, but the development of Sandia Labs, Kirtland Air Force Base, and the Albuquerque Airport curtailed urban growth to the south.

The Federal Highway Act that created Interstate 40 to replace all of Route 66 also created the north-south Interstate 25 through the middle of the state. The two interstates were planned to intersect in Albuquerque. The first portion of Interstate 40 was built north of Old Town. The entire project for both interstates, with a major multi-tiered interchange (known locally as the "Big I") was completed in 1970. Fourth Street in particular, as well as Central Avenue and Route 66 in general, seemed doomed to oblivion.

But Route 66 refused to disappear. John Steinbeck's *The Grapes of Wrath*, Bobby Troup's *Get Your Kicks on Route 66*, and TV characters Buzz and Tod, with their Corvette, have frozen the highway into America's collective memory.

Today, on Central Avenue, between Tramway Road and 98th Street, about forty motels dating to 1955 or earlier are still open. One of the most picturesque and active areas with shops, cafés, galleries, and nightspots reminiscent of the Route 66 era is Nob Hill, east of the University of New Mexico campus. Through the heart of downtown, Central Avenue is busy.

To savor the heyday of Route 66, stop at the 66 Diner at 1405 Central Avenue NE. Originally a gas station, it was converted into a diner in 1987. In May 1995, it was destroyed by fire but the owner, Tom Willis, rebuilt it in 1996. It is a virtual 1950s

Left: The KiMo Theatre, built in the "Pueblo Deco" style, opened in 1927 and remains an important Albuquerque cultural landmark.

Below: Bob Myers, owner of the American International Rattlesnake Museum. The animal conservation museum has more than thirty live species on display.

time capsule, even down to the Burma Shave signs along the sidewalk.

Next door is the New Mexico Route 66 Association headquarters, headed by Vice President Tom Willis and President Andy House. The organization publishes the *Route 66 New Mexico* magazine four times a year and also sponsors a number of events, including the annual two-day New Mexico Motor Tour.

Downtown Albuquerque is a complex of government buildings, financial institutions, a civic center, and a variety of business offices. But in spite of all the changes, vestiges of Route 66 remain, such as the KiMo Theatre, opened in 1927, and Maisel's Indian Trading Post, opened in 1937.

Another area to check out is the original Old Town. The site of the original Villa de Alburquerque that was established in 1706, the plaza is dominated by the San Felipe de Neri Church, built in 1793, and several other structures that are at least two hundred years old.

Today there are around 130 shops, restaurants, and art galleries, plus a central plaza with a bandstand and replicas of two Civil War cannons left behind by the Confederates as they retreated back to Texas. Today, Old Town is more than a quaint shopping center; it is also the core of the Hispanic cultural legacy of the Albuquerque metropolitan area. Constant entertainment, dance programs, and religious festivities, especially around Christmas, keep the city's 300-year legacy alive and well.

A block west of Old Town is the Turquoise Mu-

seum. The Lowry and Zachary families have mined, cut, studied, and sold turquoise for five generations. The two families share their wealth of knowledge about this unique Southwest gemstone that is sacred to many Indian tribes.

Northeast of Old Town, the Albuquerque Museum of Art and History specializes in exhibits dealing with Southwest and Albuquerque history. And just across Mountain Road is the New Mexico Museum of Natural History and Science, where they have excellent high-tech interactive displays of past geological eras, including a lot of dinosaurs; planetarium; DynaTheater with a large, wrap-

Above: A powwow dancer at the Gathering of Nations in Albuquerque.

Right: The New Mexico state gem, turquoise, adorns this vintage Native American jewelry at the Turquoise Museum.

Far right: Hand-painted pottery is one of the many arts found at Skip Maisel's Indian Jewelry and Crafts.

Overleaf: The colorful Gathering of Nations event is one of the largest powwows in the country and promotes Native culture from more than 500 tribes.

around screen; and a constant source of activities for young people.

Across the street from Old Town on Central Avenue you'll find the Rio Grande Zoological Park, where they have more than one thousand animals representing three hundred species.

A short trip west from Old Town on Central Avenue will bring you to the Rio Grande Botanic Garden and Albuquerque Aquarium. Exhibits range from an explanation of the Rio Grande's riparian-bosque environment to a walk-through tank with a passel of sharks and other ocean species.

The Botanic Garden, with a walkway along the bank of the Rio Grande, maintains formal outdoor gardens, southwestern xeriscaping, and two splendid conservatories, one featuring plants of the lush and humid Mediterranean world, and another devoted to Sonoran Desert cacti and plants.

When you cross the Rio Grande bridge, you will find a number of motels and cafés that relate to the 1950s–60s era of Route 66. Once you pass 98th Street, the slopes of Nine-Mile Hill become more apparent.

As you cross over the crest and find the turnoff on the Atrisco Overpass, you will be back on old Route 66. The major 66 stop on the north side of the road is the Enchanted Trails RV Park & Trading Post. From 1947 to 1969 it was called the Hill Top Trading Post, and was owned by L. G. and Lena Hill. L.G.'s brother George and his wife Morene also owned the Rio Puerco Trading Post eight miles west.

The business evolved into a campground in 1969, though the new owners still sold souvenirs. When Vickie Ashcraft bought the facilities in 1987, the name had become the Enchanted Trails. Besides the convenience store, there is a gift shop and museum featuring Route 66 memorabilia and an RV Park with spaces for travelers with trailers.

A '50 Hudson Commodore pulls "Evelyn," a '54 VaKaShunette trailer at the Enchanted Trails RV Park & Trading Post.

Right: The Sandia Peak Aerial Tramway, one of the longest of its kind in the world, will take you on a stunning ride to the 10,360-foot (3,158 m) peak of the Sandia Mountains.

And a dozen 1960s-era campers and vintage Airstream trailers can be rented out on a nightly basis. A large percentage of her business comes from foreign "roadies," mostly from Europe, who are fascinated by pre-World War II Americana.

Continuing west, it's primarily downhill for the remaining six miles into the valley of the Rio Puerco. The original Rio Puerco Trading Post burned down in 1946. George and Morene Hill built a new trading post, which included the Rio Puerco Animal Land, exhibiting local animals. That building burned down in the late 1960s and the site is presently occupied by a Travel Plaza, gas station, and convenience store.

Old-timers might remember when the Rio Puerco Animal Land entrance was flanked by a glass-enclosed stuffed polar bear. This was the last thing travelers expected to find in the New Mexico landscape. To the nearby Canyoncito Navajos, however, bears are sacred and not to be hunted, much less stuffed and put on public display. One night someone broke the glass case and spirited the stuffed bear away. It was later found on the high slope of the Sandia Mountains, completely torn to pieces.

Here are some other attractions in the Albuquerque area, not necessarily related to Route 66. Contact information can be found in the back of the book.

Sandia Peak is northeast of Albuquerque. At 10,360 feet (3,158 m) above sea level, the Peak affords an 11,000-square-mile (28,490 km^2) panoramic view of western New Mexico. Highway 14 in the western edge of Tijeras Canyon will take you

on an 11-mile scenic trip to the top. Or you can take Tramway Boulevard to the Sandia Tram Base Terminal office. The tram runs year-round and offers a ride on one of the world's longest tramways for its 2.7-mile trip to the top. Summer and fall visits to Sandia Peak afford bike and hiking trails and spectacular sunsets. Winter and early spring trips provide an opportunity to ski at the longest cruising terrain available in New Mexico, including thirty trails serviced by four chairlifts.

Because the Atomic Age was born in New Mexico, the National Museum of Nuclear Science & History has a fascinating story to tell—from the World War II Manhattan Project at Los Alamos to the role of Sandia Labs and Kirtland Air Force Base. This museum has high-tech exhibits and quality educational programs.

Below: The Tinkertown Museum features miniature, hand-carved figures in scenes that animate at the push of a button. This circus sideshow is among dozens of elaborate exhibits created over forty years by the museum's late founder Ross Ward.

Between Louisiana and San Pedro Avenues is the New Mexico State Fairgrounds. Built in 1936, the complex of buildings hosts the annual State Fair for fourteen days in early September. Other activities throughout the year include conventions, art festivals, rock concerts, and flea markets.

The University of New Mexico has several facilities that are open to the public. The University Art Museum has the fifth-largest collection of photographs in the country. Gallery space is also devoted to fine art and Spanish Colonial artifacts. The Maxwell Museum of Anthropology explores Southwestern history and culture, and permanent exhibits describe the various groups that have made this area their home over the past 11,000 years. The Museum of Southwestern Biology offers tours highlighting the biodiversity of the Southwestern United States.

North of Central Avenue on 12th Street is the Indian Pueblo Cultural Center. Operated by the All-Indian Pueblo Council, representing nineteen Pueblos, the center provides an excellent introduction to Southwest Indian peoples and their unique creative, historical, and social worlds.

Albuquerque's signature annual event is the International Balloon Fiesta. The first organized fiesta was held in 1973 with 138 balloons. The 9-day fiesta, held in early October, now accommodates around 900 balloons and is the biggest event of its kind in the world. Balloon Fiesta Park is the site of all the balloon ascensions. Nearby you can also visit the Anderson-Abruzzo Albuquerque International Balloon Museum.

Another event at Balloon Fiesta Park is the annual, three-day Celtic Festival in mid-May, featuring highland games, music, ethnic foods, and other events that relate to an Irish, Scottish, and Welsh legacy.

Finally, check out Petroglyph National Monument along the Rio Grande valley's west rim to learn about the seventeen-mile-long lava escarpment and the five volcanic cinder cones, as well as the more than 15,000 prehistoric petroglyphs that have been found in that region.

Follow the story of the Atomic Age at the National Museum of Nuclear Science & History. Exhibits include replicas of the two nuclear bombs, Little Boy and Fat Man, that helped end World War II.

Right: The Anderson-Abruzzo Albuquerque International Balloon Museum, located near the Balloon Fiesta Park, is committed to advancing and maintaining the history, adventure, culture, and science of ballooning.

Visit the Unser Racing Museum for multiple generations of racing history, cars, and memorabilia. The Unser family has nine Indianapolis 500 victories.

GRAF ZEPPELIN

The World
Changed Forever

In 1785 man freed himself from the confines of gravity
with the invention of flight. In that year, both hot air
and gas balloons were invented near Paris, France.

The Arena
of the Future

Side Trip

LOS LUNAS

This side trip is meant to follow the original, pre-1937 Route 66 roadway that circumvented the hazardous Rio Puerco arroyo. It's fairly easy to trace, with many road signs stating that this is the pre-1937 Historic Route 66.

Starting at Central Avenue and 4th Street, go south on 4th to Bridge Boulevard. Consider visiting the National Hispanic Cultural Center at this intersection. It is a center for the study of all things Hispanic and features art and historical exhibit areas, library, genealogy center, performing arts theater, and many seasonal activities.

Back at the intersection of Bridge Boulevard, travel west, cross the bridge over the Rio Grande, and at the intersection (mile 2.1) turn left on Isleta Boulevard. For the next twenty miles or so you will also be traveling on the original Camino Real. About a mile farther along (mile 3.5), bear left and stay on Isleta Boulevard.

After eleven miles, you will pass under I-25, and you also enter the Isleta Pueblo Reservation. Isleta Boulevard becomes Highway 314. After another two-and-a-half miles, you come to junction 147, which takes you into the plaza of Isleta Pueblo.

The pueblo dates back to the fourteenth century. In the late summer of 1540, the pueblo was briefly visited by a group of Spaniards under Captain Hernando de Alvarado of the Coronado expedition. It came under Spanish influence shortly after the establishment of Santa Fe and the St. Anthony Church was completed in 1613.

During the aftermath of the Pueblo Revolt of 1680, most of the church was destroyed. Then in the late 1690s, Spanish control was reestablished throughout the Rio Grande pueblos, including Isleta. The mission church was rebuilt in 1716 and dedicated to St. Augustine.

Today Isleta is a friendly, prosperous town of 3,000 residents, on a reservation of 211,000 acres that straddles the Rio Grande. Its main enterprise is the Isleta Hotel & Casino. The pueblo also runs the championship 27-hole Eagle Golf Course and the Isleta Lakes and RV Park.

Back on Highway 314 and continuing south, some twenty miles beyond Central Avenue, you will reach the community of Los Lunas. Turn right on Main Street/Highway 6 and go past the Luna-Otero Mansion and continue west.

The next thirty-four miles on Highway 6 traces the original Route 66 in its effort to evade the steep Rio Puerco arroyo, which flows through a rather broad valley as it reaches its convergence with the Rio Grande.

Right before the turn in the highway that will lead to the remnants of Correo, there is a Laguna Pueblo housing project with a convenience store. Today, Correo is a ghost town. The only things still standing are the signs that used to identify Highland Meadows Trading Post and Wild Horse Mesa Bar.

At mile 56, you will be at the end of Highway 6, and at the junction of I-40, which basically overlays the former Route 66. You are no longer off the beaten path.

Left: Agriculture is a long-standing tradition in the Middle Rio Grande Valley.

Above: The supposedly haunted Luna-Otero Mansion, completed in 1881, was built by the Santa Fe Railway as a gift for allowing the railroad access through the Luna property. The building is on the National Register of Historic Places and is now a family owned fine dining restaurant.

Right: Connie Hatley with her miniature pony, Silverado, at the VIVA New Mexico Chile Festival held in Los Lunas each year in September.

LAND OF THE PUEBLOS

ALBUQUERQUE (RIO PUERCO) TO M^cCARTYS

IN THE PREVIOUS CHAPTER, you find yourself about seventeen miles west of Albuquerque and approaching the arroyo (small canyon) of the Rio Puerco of the East. This chapter begins with a piece of new technology superimposed on a land of ancient cultures—the Parker truss bridge.

The Parker truss bridge was erected in 1933. Its 250-foot span is one of the longest in New Mexico. This structure was replaced by the new nearby Interstate 40 bridge, and in 1999 was restricted to all automobile traffic. It is now on the National Register of Historic Sites and is being preserved by the New Mexico State Highway Department.

Once you've crossed over to the Rio Puerco's west side, you enter the Laguna Pueblo Indian Reservation. On the south side of I-40 is a cluster of buildings, including a five-story hotel named the Route 66 Casino Hotel, which is owned and maintained by the Laguna Pueblo.

From this point until you get to Mesita, the interstate follows the original Route 66. About ten miles west of the Route 66 Casino Hotel is a turnoff to the north (Trail 56) that leads to the community of Cañoncito. This is a small reservation of Navajos who had accommodated eighteenth- and early nineteenth-century Spanish and Mexican settlers. However, the Navajos ended up going on the infamous Long Walk to Fort Sumner (1863–1868) too. Today they refer to their reservation as To'hajiilee.

Five miles farther along is the 126 overpass. This connects with Highway 6, which will take you to Los Lunas.

Continuing west on the interstate, take the off-ramp at the 117 overpass at Mesita. Mesita was founded around 1880 by Laguna tribal members who were unhappy with the Pueblo leadership. Conservative "defectors" included traditional medicine men and their followers who found it difficult to accept Protestant missionaries in the main pueblo.

If you take a rather quick left turn after the overpass, follow signs to Highway 124 and to an old paved two-lane road, which is the original Route 66. A couple miles later, the parallel interstate veers off to the left and up a hill. Route 66 continues north, past a large lava outcrop known as Owl Rock and then sharply bends around the base of a cliff called Dead Man's Curve. A mile or so later, this road also bears to the left and begins a steep climb to the mesa top. Once you've reached the summit, the Pueblo of San José de Laguna sprawls out before you.

Left: The San José de la Laguna Mission and Convento at Laguna Pueblo was built in 1699.

Right: Dead Man's Curve near Laguna Pueblo.

Although this area has been inhabited by Ancestral Pueblo people for nearly a thousand years, Laguna (Ka'waika) is technically the newest of all the Southwest pueblos. Groups of Keresan-speaking farmers inhabited this region for centuries before the Spaniards came.

When the Spaniards, under Juan de Oñate, began to settle the upper Rio Grande and exert control over the New Mexico pueblos in 1598, this area was overlooked because it did not consist of a singular, cohesive village. There wasn't much of an effect on the region (compared to Acoma, Zuni, and the Hopi villages) during the Pueblo Revolt of 1680. However, when the Spaniards returned in force in 1693, things began to change. The reconquest of northern New Mexico was a three-year bloody affair, and many at the Rio Grande pueblos took refuge. Some went to the Navajos, and some went to the Hopis. Those who spoke Keresan from Cochiti, Santo Domingo, Zia, and Cieneguilla fled to the Laguna area.

Antagonisms eventually diminished, and in 1699 Spanish officials recognized the pueblo near the lake and built the mission San José (St. Joseph) on the river of the same name, dedicating it on July 4, 1701. The influx of refugees from various Rio Grande pueblos made this pueblo a melting pot of Southwestern Indian culture. And because Spaniards visited Laguna from the start, Hispanic and Catholic influence also played a role in defining its unique culture. This may explain why there are still some traditional religious practices and ceremonies but an absence of any kivas or major religious societies.

Throughout the eighteenth century, the population of Laguna grew, even as the lake dried up, and eventually five satellite farming villages were founded: Seama, Encinal, Paguate, Paraje, and Mesita. Each of these villages has its own chapel and celebrates its own Feast Day dedicated to its patron saint.

Traditionally, their economy was based on farming and stock-raising. But a uranium mining operation in the 1960s and '70s made Laguna a relatively wealthy tribe. Consequently, few artisans are still active, and the pueblo contains no trading posts or tourist facilities, although visitors are always welcome. (Note that the pueblo has restrictions on cameras, tape recorders, and sketch pads, especially during religious festivities.) Today the population of Laguna and its suburbs is about 7,000 people.

At the village of Paraje there is a junction with state Highway 23. This road will take you to the

Above: Laguna Pueblo is overlooked by the Pueblo-Franciscan style mission, with Mount Taylor, one of the four sacred peaks to the region's Native Americans, in the background.

Below: Sink your teeth into a world-famous Laguna Burger at the 66 Pit Stop.

interstate and the 108 overpass. On the south side of the interstate is the Dancing Eagle Casino. But you can stay on Highway 23 heading south for one of two ways to reach Acoma, the Sky City.

If you stay on Highway 124 and head west, you'll come to one of the most intriguing spots on the entire route—Budville.

In the 1920s, Roscoe Rice had a garage in the area, and when Route 66 was built, his garage was right on the highway. His son Howard Rice eventually took over the business. Everybody called Howard "Bud," and in the late '30s he named the place after himself, Budville. Bud and his wife Flossie expanded the business to include a towing and wrecking service, a gas station, general store, Greyhound Bus stop, and a courtroom. Bud became the justice of the peace for the area as well as the local vendor for license plates and driver's licenses. Flossie acted as deputy sheriff. Their tow trucks were the only ones that operated between Rio Puerco and Grants.

Bud was murdered during a hold-up in 1967, but no one was ever found guilty of the crime. Gus Raney, a gun-toting former lawman and close friend of Bud, suspected Flossie's new ex-con husband. Raney took the law into his own hands and shot Flossie's second husband dead. He was never tried for the killing. In 1997, Flossie sold the wrecker and closed the towing garage.

Continuing along the original Route 66, Highway 124, you will come to the Cubero cemetery. When

Right: The cemetery at Cubero became the final resting place of three Confederate soldiers.

Below: The Budville Trading Company, a center of intrigue in the middle of nowhere.

Captain Francisco Aragon relocated his troops from Cubero to Albuquerque on March 2, 1862, Confederate General Henry Sibley sent Company A of the 7th Texas Mounted Volunteers to retrieve twenty-five wagon-loads of supplies and ammunition. Three ailing Confederates left behind were said to have died of pleurisy and were buried here. A memorial stone honoring these three men was dedicated at the site in December 2002. To our knowledge, this is the only original Confederate burial place on the entire route.

The original site of nearby Cubero was occupied by a group of Keresan pueblo farmers, who were relocated to Laguna in 1699. Spanish governor Pedro Rodriguez Cubero had negotiated the concentration of Keresan groups into the village of Laguna, and when Spanish ranchers eventually settled in the area, they named it Villa de Cubero. During the American period, a supply depot for the army was established at Cubero, and when Fort Lyon was abandoned at the outbreak of the Civil War, all the inventory of supplies, food, and ammunition was placed in the Cubero warehouses.

On the outskirts of the community stands a gas station and convenience store flanked by a shuttered-up motel. It is said that Ernest Hemingway stayed here in the early 1950s to write his masterpiece, *The Old Man and the Sea*.

A few miles northwest lies the village of San Fidel. During the days of Route 66, there were a number of saloons or cafés here, namely Tafoya's Café, Ray's Bar, and Charlie Shook's Trading Post, all now abandoned. The White Arrow Garage and the Acoma Curio Shop are also shut down, but a Catholic mission school, a chapel bearing painted blue angels, and a nearby winery help the town maintain some vitality. A road that runs due south for a couple of miles ends at the interstate and connects with the Acoma Pueblo–owned Sky City Casino, restaurant, and hotel.

Running south from the casino (Exit 102) is Highway 32, which passes through Acomita and is an alternative route to Acoma Pueblo (see Side Trip). A terrific feature at the Sky City Casino is the large mural depicting the history of Route 66.

If you travel about two miles west of San Fidel on Highway 124, you will come to the dilapidated remains of Chief's Rancho—a restaurant, bar, curio store, motel, and service station. Ely House Jr., the first chief of the New Mexico State Police, built it when he retired in 1944.

The service station was one of a chain organized by Arthur Whiting and his three brothers, who previously owned a gas station in St. Johns, Arizona. Starting in 1926, they expanded into a chain of stations and motels from California to Oklahoma. The earlier signs advertising their service stations were fifty feet long and six feet high, painted bright yellow with red letters.

According to Arthur Whiting, their expansion started with the Ford dealer in Holbrook, Arizona. They took on the Union Oil Company as commission agents, but when the independent gasoline business opened up in New Mexico, they dropped Union and began trucking lucrative wholesale gasoline out of New Mexico.

The Whitings kept building stations and motels, and their customers kept coming down Route 66, even during the Depression. Through the end of World War II, they sold their gas for twenty cents a gallon.

Just beyond Chief's Rancho Café, the highway will take you over I-40 at exit 96 and into McCartys. The village is one of Acoma Pueblo's outliers, and was named after the contractor who occupied the site during the railroad's construction.

The most prominent sight in McCartys is the Santa Maria de Acoma Church, built in 1933, that overlooks the village and Route 66. Famed Southwest architect John Gaw Meem designed the church in Pueblo Mission style, and as a one-half scale replica of the Acoma mission, San Estevan del Rey. Made of local rock, it is a beautiful example of Pueblo people blending characteristics of the traditional Catholic and Native American faiths and beliefs. The annual Santa Maria Feast Day is held on the first Sunday in May and is open to the public.

When you leave McCartys on the original route, it winds and curves along the contour of cliffs that line the Rio San Jose. When it crosses this river on an old Parker truss bridge, you are a mile from the overpass at I-40, Exit 89.

For many years, especially right after the end of World War II, all along the route from Mesita to Exit 89, Laguna and Acoma potters maintained shaded arbors along the side of the road where they sold their handmade pottery. There was little difference then in the pottery designs offered by artisans of either pueblo.

A story goes that the enterprising young daughter of a potter collected cocklebur seed pods, which she sold to the tourists as rare "porcupine eggs." And the tourists bought them!

Above: The Santa Maria de Acoma Church, built in 1933 and designed by John Gaw Meem, overlooks Route 66 in McCartys.

Right: Kasha-Katuwe Tent Rocks National Monument. Kasha-Katuwe means "white cliffs" in the Keresan language of Cochiti Pueblo.

Side Trip

ACOMA PUEBLO

This side trip has two routes. You can go back and forth from Interstate 40 on either one, or travel to Acoma on one route, and then return by the other. The two routes are Highway 23 (from the 108 exit) and Highway 32 (from the 102 exit). Highway 23 is an eleven-mile trip to Acoma. Highway 32 takes a little longer but goes through Acomita. Its classic mission church of San Lorenzo was built in 1888 but renovated in 1939 and rededicated to Santa Ana (Feast Day is August 10).

The impressive Acoma Pueblo is considered the oldest continuously occupied town in the United States. Both pottery sherds and tree-ring dates indicate that its first inhabitants began to construct some of the house blocks in the twelfth century. These people spoke Keresan and referred to themselves as "A'kome"— people of the white rock. Acoma sits atop a sheer-walled mesa 370 feet above the surrounding countryside. It's not hard to imagine how it obtained its nickname "Sky City."

In 1540, the Spanish government explored the northern regions in search of the fabled golden Cities of Cibola. The commander of this expedition, Don Francisco Vasquez de Coronado, and an advance force of some seventy-five cavaliers, infantry, and Indian allies, made first contact with the Pueblo Indians when they attacked the Zuni village of Hawikku.

Acoma pottery.

While occupying Hawikku to await the main contingent, Coronado sent out exploratory parties. One group commanded by Captain Hernando de Alvarado was sent east to contact the pueblos located along a large river. On September 3, 1540, Alvarado and his men arrived at Acoma Pueblo. The village elders met him at the base of the mesa with food and buffalo hides. After exchanging gifts, Alvarado was invited to climb the stairway to the mesa top. He later wrote in his report, "This site is one of the strongest ever seen, because the city is built upon a very high rock. The ascent was so difficult that we repented climbing to the top. The houses are three to four stories high. The people are of the same type as those in the province of Cibola [Zuni], and they have abundant supplies of maize, beans, and turkeys like those of New Spain [Mexico]."

For the next half century, Acoma was not visited by any other Spanish expeditions. Things began to change drastically for the fifty-eight pueblos in the summer of 1598. Don Juan de Oñate, the new governor of the northern province of Nuevo Mexico, led over three hundred settlers into the area, established the colony of San Gabriel del Yunque, and visited all the pueblos and demanded their loyalty and obedience to the king of Spain.

In late November, Oñate visited Acoma and received a cold reception but managed to elicit a pledge of loyalty to the Spanish king. He then continued his trip to the Zuni pueblos.

Two weeks later, Oñate's nephew, Juan de Zaldivar, and sixteen soldiers stopped at Acoma, demanding food and blankets. The Acoma leaders decided that enough was enough. They enticed Zaldivar and thirteen of his soldiers to climb up to the pueblo on top of the mesa for a meal. Once they gained the summit, Acoma warriors killed Zaldivar and his men. The survivors quickly rode to Zuni to report to Oñate.

Back at San Gabriel, Oñate and his colonists suffered through a somber and gloomy Christmas. Oñate had few options for keeping the colony from being overrun or abandoned. One-sixth of his fighting force had been killed at Acoma, reinforcements were eight hundred miles away, and it was the dead of winter. He decided that they must chastise and punish Acoma with all the resources available, or other pueblos would take a similar stance against the Spaniards.

On January 12, 1599, seventy heavily armed men commanded by Vicente de Zaldivar, the slain Juan's brother, returned to the pueblo and demanded that the warriors responsible for the attack surrender. With no response, Zaldivar placed the mesa under siege. That night, a handful of men with a cannon managed to climb up to the pueblo's south side. After a three-day battle, eight hundred Acomans had been killed. Many inhabitants escaped, but six hundred captives were taken to Santo Domingo Pueblo to stand trial. Men over twenty-five years of age were sentenced to twenty years of servitude, and about two dozen had one foot amputated. Elderly men and women were distributed to other pueblos and Plains Indians to be used as servants. A group of teenaged girls was sent to a convent in Mexico City, but most of the younger children were released without punishment. To Oñate, the retaliation and severe punishment seemed to work, and no major problems with the pueblos occurred until 1680.

By 1603, the Acomans had rebuilt most of the house blocks, and the pueblo was an active community once again.

In 1629, the Father Custodian of the Franciscans, Fray Esteban de Perea, decided to extend their missionary endeavors out to the western pueblos. On June 23, a well-equipped party, including Governor Don Francisco Manuel de Silva Nieto, set out from Santa Fe.

White ladders rest against Acoma Pueblo.

Their first stop was at Acoma. The Pueblo leaders finally allowed Fray Christobal Juan Ramirez and several soldiers to take up residence and supervise the construction of a church. The construction of the church, convento (living quarters for the priest), and cemetery on top of the mesa at Acoma turned out to be an awesome task.

The massive mission still stands on its original construction site, with mud and stone walls that are 9 feet thick and nearly 60 feet high. The church alone is 150 feet long and 40 feet wide. Fray Ramirez built a better road to the mesa top so that burros could transport huge loads of building materials. The great logs for the roof vigas, over 40 feet long, were cut from ponderosa pine trees in the Cebolleta Mountains thirty miles away.

Climbing the ancient stairway to Acoma Pueblo.

Shortly thereafter, the king of Spain presented to the mission a large oil painting of Saint Joseph holding the Christ child. It survived the Pueblo Revolt and was the center of controversy when the Acomans loaned it to the Pueblo of Laguna, who then refused to give it back. In 1855 the new American Territorial Court decreed that the painting be returned to Acoma. Today it is perhaps the most prized Spanish artifact in any New Mexico pueblo.

Acoma participated with all the other pueblos in the Pueblo Revolt of 1680, led by the San Juan medicine man, Po'Pay, or Popé. On August 10, Acoma murdered Fray Luis Maldonado Olasqueain, the priest in residence. In all, the Indians killed nearly five hundred Spaniards, including twenty-one priests, and destroyed many churches and ranches. The surviving Spaniards fled to El Paso del Norte (El Paso, Texas).

In 1693, Don Diego de Vargas began the reconquest of this northern province of Nuevo Mexico. In 1699, Acoma and the Pueblo of San José de Laguna formally submitted to Spanish rule. The mission was restored, and Spaniards introduced horses, cattle, sheep, fruit trees, and new customs. A more accommodating Catholic faith allowed traditional ceremonies and rituals to be incorporated into church events. This amalgamation of Spanish and Indian cultures is uniquely characteristic of New Mexico today.

The Acoma reservation comprises 431,600 acres, and the current population is estimated at more than 4,800, but only a dozen or so families reside permanently in the mesa-top village.

The history, family traditions, and cultural heritage of the Acoma people are highlighted at the new Sky City Cultural Center located near the base of Acoma mesa. The center includes the Haak'u Museum, a theater, the Y'aak'a restaurant, which serves a variety of Native foods, and the Gaits'i Gift Shop. For generations, Acoma artisans have made fine, thin-walled pottery, distinctive with its white slip and designs in dark brown or black, red, yellows, tan, or orange.

CHAPTER 6

BADLANDS AND CARROTS

McCARTYS TO GRANTS TO THE CONTINENTAL DIVIDE

FOR DECADES, travelers on Route 66 encountered more variety of land and people in New Mexico than in any other segment of the entire route. When you approach the overpass at mile 89, you leave Pueblo country and enter a region rocked by the cataclysmic forces of volcano eruptions.

The dominant feature on the northern horizon is Mount Taylor. Named after President Zachary Taylor by the invading American forces during the War with Mexico in 1846, it is also called Tsoodzil by the Navajos, who consider it to be their sacred mountain to the south. Although it reigns in quiet beauty now, it was a fiery caldron of volcanic activity three million years ago.

Eruptions around 750,000 years ago produced lava flows that compose El Malpais (Spanish for The Badlands). El Calderon Volcano erupted about 115,000 years ago, and the Bandera Volcano erupted 11,000 years ago. The most recent volcanic activity occurred only 3,000 years ago when McCarty's Crater sent lava flows almost forty miles to the north, filling in portions of the Rio San Jose basin. El Malpais National Monument and Conservation Area comprises more than 378,000 acres of lava rock, cinder cones, shield volcanoes, caves, and deep lava tubes.

At the 89 overpass, take Highway 117 south nine miles to El Malpais Ranger Station. Another mile takes you to the awesome raw lava flows and cinder cones at Sandstone Bluffs Overlook. Eight miles

farther south is the viewpoint at one of New Mexico's largest sandstone arches. High in the cliffs, La Ventana Natural Arch is a beautiful example of the powerful erosive forces that have carved up the Colorado Plateau.

Back at the 89 overpass, you can stay on the interstate or continue on Highway 117 North and follow the old right-of-way of Route 66 to Grants. When 117 turns into Santa Fe Avenue, make a left turn and approach Exit 85 on the interstate. Continue on the overpass and go south for a quarter mile until you reach the Northwest New Mexico Visitor Center, where you'll find a small archaeology exhibit.

Left: La Ventana Natural Arch, New Mexico's second tallest arch, frames the sky in El Malpais National Conservation Area.

Right: The Sandstone Bluffs overlook in El Malpais National Monument, with Mount Taylor in the distance.

Return to Santa Fe Avenue and travel along Route 66 through Grants. Grants began in the 1880s as a base camp for men building the Atlantic and Pacific Railroad (Atchison, Topeka and Santa Fe Railway). Three brothers—John, Angus, and Lewis Grant—provided supply inventories and cut timbers from the nearby Zuni Mountains to be used for railroad ties.

In 1950, a Navajo rancher, Paddy Martinez, found some funny-looking yellow rocks around his sheep camp near Haystack Mountain. They contained uranium oxide from the Jurassic-age Morrison Formation, which has most of the uranium resources found in the Grants-Gallup area.

Left: This weathered neon sign that once advertised the Grants Motel has been demolished since the photo was taken.

Right: The Grants Café neon sign has been restored.

Above: Relive the experience of uranium miners in the New Mexico Mining Museum's underground mine exhibit.

Right: Franciscan Lodge postcard from the Route 66 postcard display at Cibola Arts Council's Double Six Gallery.

From 1951 until the mid-'70s, Grants was the home of big-time mining and milling operations. Every business along Santa Fe Avenue was open and thriving. Traveling this street today can give you the impression that Grants is a bleak and unlovely place. But once you turn off this street, you will find tree-lined avenues, shopping centers, and neat schoolyards, including a branch campus of New Mexico State University.

On the east portion of Santa Fe Avenue, there are reminders of the Route 66 era. The 34-unit Franciscan Lodge that opened in 1950 with the motto, "The Best Costs No More," is now closed. The Grants Café, which opened in 1937, is also closed, but its large sign with the red arrow has been restored and preserved.

Just west of the town center is the Mission Gallery and Lewis Fine Art Studio. Mike Lewis has turned an old church into a gallery featuring his own art. A block away is the Uranium Café, which was a popular stopping place during the heyday of Route 66 but is now closed.

On the west side of Riverside Park is the New Mexico Mining Museum, a big building with mining equipment scattered across the front lawn. The museum's main floor tells the story of the uranium-mining industry that was so central to Grants for a quarter-century, and the exhibits are well designed and informative. And there is a life-size replica of a working uranium mine on the lower level.

A couple of blocks farther west on Santa Fe Avenue is the Cibola Arts Council's Double Six Gallery and Cibola Art and Artifacts Museum. The Double Six Gallery is a permanent display of more than fifty postcards, all relating to Route 66 and enlarged to 24" × 18" panels. The postcards, dating back to the 1930s through 1960s, depict scenes from Laguna Pueblo to the Continental Divide.

On the west side of Grants, at Exit 81, you have several options. One is to access Highway 53 and drive south through the quaint Hispanic settlement of San Rafael and along the western edge of El Malpais lava field. There are picnic-area stops, El Calderon site, El Malpais Information Center, and the Bandera Crater and Ice Caves. Not only can you hike to the top of Bandera Volcano and look down into the 750-foot-deep crater but you can also descend into a natural lava tube, where collected rainwater freezes in the winter but because of the lava-insulation never melts in the summer.

This combination of fire and ice lent its name to the Fire and Ice Bike Rally held in Grants every year for the past fifteen years. That rally is being replaced by a Route 66 fiesta and car show the third weekend in July. Also try for the Route 66 Fall Fiesta held in Grants every second weekend of October.

Meanwhile, back to Exit 81, where you have another option. This one follows the road signs to the Grants-Milan airport and the adjacent Aviation Heritage Museum. The Mother Road acted as a map for pilots flying cross-country between Los Angeles, California, and Amarillo, Texas.

Early in the twentieth century, pilots followed the railroad and the parallel roads that became Route 66 and flew only during daylight. The Mid-Continental Airway, designed by Charles Lindbergh in 1929, was a series of lit beacons between Albuquerque and the Arizona border. This system allowed pilots to fly at night, and continued its vital service until World War II, by which time the beacons were replaced by radar and other technologies. Today, the only functioning beacon left is at the Grants Aviation Heritage Museum.

Back again to Exit 81. Your final option is to stay on Santa Fe Avenue and drive westward into the

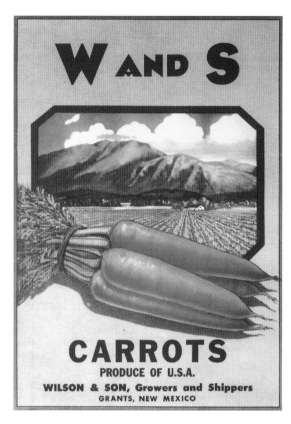

The carrots on this Double Six Gallery poster were a major local crop.

Right: A 1929 55-foot beacon tower and concrete arrow pointed the way for pilots. Lovingly restored by the Western New Mexico Aviation Heritage Museum.

town of Milan, named for Mexican refugee Salvador Milán. The refugees were among the hundreds of farmers and laborers who worked the expansive carrot fields throughout the valley, stretching twelve miles west of Grants. These carrots were shipped to retail outlets throughout the western United States until 1953, when the water that had been allocated for irrigation was redirected to new uranium processing mills northwest of Milan. Unfortunately, even after the uranium boom ended in the mid-'70s, the carrot fields never returned.

As you proceed west through Milan, Santa Fe Avenue becomes Route 66 for a while. At the outskirts of Milan, the road is Highway 122 all the way to the Continental Divide.

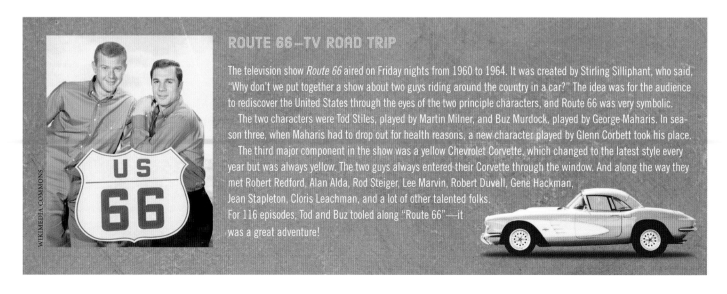

ROUTE 66—TV ROAD TRIP

The television show *Route 66* aired on Friday nights from 1960 to 1964. It was created by Stirling Silliphant, who said, "Why don't we put together a show about two guys riding around the country in a car?" The idea was for the audience to rediscover the United States through the eyes of the two principle characters, and Route 66 was very symbolic.

The two characters were Tod Stiles, played by Martin Milner, and Buz Murdock, played by George Maharis. In season three, when Maharis had to drop out for health reasons, a new character played by Glenn Corbett took his place.

The third major component in the show was a yellow Chevrolet Corvette, which changed to the latest style every year but was always yellow. The two guys always entered their Corvette through the window. And along the way they met Robert Redford, Alan Alda, Rod Steiger, Lee Marvin, Robert Duvall, Gene Hackman, Jean Stapleton, Cloris Leachman, and a lot of other talented folks.

For 116 episodes, Tod and Buz tooled along "Route 66"—it was a great adventure!

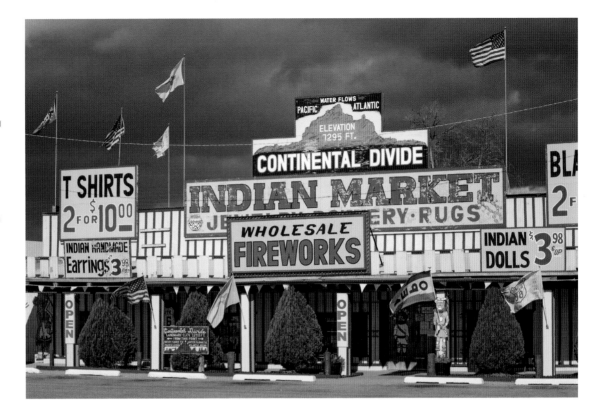

Left: Roy T. Herman's Garage and Service Station in Thoreau is one of the oldest gas stations left on Route 66.

Right: The Continental Divide Indian Market has a sign out front marking the division point where water flows either one way or the other to the Pacific and Atlantic oceans.

After leaving Milan, Highway 122 intersects the turnoff to Bluewater Lake Village gas station and curio shop, located on the nearby interstate. But stay on the original Route 66 and observe the many old, dilapidated places of business that functioned during the 1940s through the 1970s. You'll see remnants of trading posts, motor courts, gas stations, garages, and the Rattlesnake Trading Post, competition of the nearby House of Cobras. On display at the Rattlesnake Trading Post was a skeleton of a 48-foot-long "giant prehistoric reptile." Owner Jake Atkinson's monster was made out of a number of cow vertebrae and plaster, with a horn glued onto a skull that was actually made out of a cow hip.

Below: The House of Cobras postcard from the Double Six Gallery.

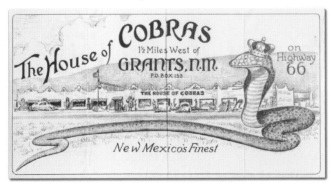

After rounding a bend, you arrive at Prewitt, where most of the roadside businesses are still

operating. This is the home of the Bi-County Fair (Cibola and McKinley counties), which is held on the first weekend of September, with animal competitions, quilting exhibits, a rodeo, and old-time fiddle contests. On the west side of town, near the Tomahawk Bar, is the railroad crossing that will take you a couple of miles north to the Casamero ruins.

Continuing west on 122, the next village is Thoreau (named after Henry David Thoreau, but pronounced by the locals as "threw"). As you get to the main access off the interstate, there is the Red Mountain Market and Johnnie's Inn bar, the only still-operating businesses remaining from the days of Route 66. At this juncture you can take Highway 612 south nine miles to Bluewater Lake State Park, or you can drive north on Highway 371 through Thoreau and on to Chaco Culture National Historical Park (see Side Trip).

As you continue out of Thoreau, the ascent is gradual, and soon you find yourself at the top of the hill, in the parking lot of Indian Market. This is the Continental Divide, the highest point on Route 66, and the end of this chapter. Ever since you turned off the interstate at Exit 89, for forty-two uninterrupted miles, you've driven the original Route 66.

CHACO CULTURE NATIONAL HISTORICAL PARK

At Exit 53 on the interstate, by Red Mountain Market and Johnnie's Inn, or on Highway 122 (original Route 66), drive north on Highway 371 over the railroad tracks, through Thoreau to Smith Lake. Going past Smith Lake, you drop down through the dramatic red rocks via Satan Pass, and twenty-five miles out of Thoreau you come to the Navajo community of Crownpoint. The Crownpoint Elementary School is the site of the world's largest Navajo rug auction, usually held the second Friday of each month.

The last eighteen miles into Chaco Canyon is an unpaved road that is seldom graded. This final stretch is NOT recommended for mobile homes or camping trailers, especially during the rainy season or after a winter snowstorm.

Proceed north out of Crownpoint for about five miles to the junction with Tribal Route 9. Take this paved road east for about eleven miles to Seven Lakes. There's an abandoned trading post here and the junction with State Highway 57 (Tribal Route 14). This eighteen-mile stretch of dirt can be impassable during bad weather. The ruts and washboards are all worth it, though, when you finally reach the visitor center at Chaco Culture National Historical Park.

If you are interested in astronomy, ask about the Chaco Night Sky Program. Leading out from the visitor center is a paved 10-mile-loop drive to most of the "great houses" along the north side of Chaco Canyon, and the great, or communal, kiva on the south side.

Chaco Canyon, the major riparian system draining the central part of the San Juan Basin, seems an unlikely place for prehistoric Ancestral Pueblo people to develop and nurture a major cultural and architectural center. This is high desert country, with long winters, short growing seasons, and marginal rainfall. Yet, a thousand years ago, this shallow canyon was the center of community life, agriculture, commerce, and ceremony. Although the Ancestral Pueblo culture extended over the entire southern half of the Colorado Plateau, the inhabitants of Chaco built monumental masonry and timber buildings, which were connected by a network of roads to as many as 150 outlying communities. In architecture, complexity of community life, social organization, religious rituals, and regional trade and integration, the people of Chaco attained a unique cultural expression and status unmatched anywhere in prehistoric North America.

This cultural flowering of the Chacoan people began in the mid AD 800s and lasted nearly four hundred years. Using masonry techniques unique for their time, they constructed massive multiple story stone buildings, with hundreds of rooms and numerous kivas. The buildings were planned, with foundations conceived to support four or five stories. Construction of these buildings spanned decades and even centuries. Although each great house is unique, they all face south, thus maximizing the winter sun and minimizing the summer sun.

During the middle and late 800s, the great houses of Una Vida, Pueblo Bonito, and Penasco Blanco were built. By the 900s, Hungo Pavi, Chetro Ketl, and Pueblo del Arroyo were started, with Casa Rinconada, the large kiva on the south side of the canyon, and Pueblo Alto on the north side soon being added to the complex of buildings. Sophisticated astronomical alignments indicate that these structures were often oriented to solar, lunar, planet, and cardinal directions, hinting at the depth of knowledge possessed by these ancient residents.

Doorways in Pueblo Bonito, the most well-known great house in Chaco Culture National Historical Park.

Remains of Pueblo Bonito as seen from Alto Mesa.

Besides complex social and agricultural networks, Chaco was the hub of an extensive trading and distribution system. Raw turquoise from the Cerrillos Hills mines was made into beads, ornaments, and jewelry at Chaco, and traded throughout the Southwest and northern Mexico for macaws and other parrots, copper bells, and other precious commodities. Pottery was also manufactured and traded throughout the region.

However, by the late 1100s, Chaco declined as a regional center, and groups of residents gradually migrated north to the Mesa Verde area, or east to pueblos along the Rio Grande. Other groups moved south and intermingled with the pueblo people at Acoma and Cibola (Zuni). According to folklore, some clan groups even moved west and became absorbed into the Hopi communities.

Today, almost all Pueblo groups proudly acknowledge that the blood of these Chacoan people still runs through their veins. The non-Pueblo visitor will look with amazement at what these people were able to accomplish a thousand years ago here in the high desert country of northern New Mexico.

Pueblo Bonita kivas.

CHAPTER

RED ROCK COUNTRY

CONTINENTAL DIVIDE TO GALLUP TO LUPTON

THIS FINAL LEG of our journey starts at the highest point in elevation on the entire route—the Continental Divide. At this point you are 7,263 feet (2,214 m) above sea level, and forty-seven miles east of the Arizona state line. The town here called Continental Divide used to be a thriving settlement, but all that's left now are three Indian curio shops and a gas station. A short segment of the original Route 66 parallels the present-day highway for about a mile before ending in a cul-de-sac.

Three miles down the road is a former town that went through more name changes than any other town along New Mexico's Route 66: Coolidge. The original rancher there, Billy Crane, called it Bacon Springs, but when it became a stage relay station in 1870, it became Cranes Station. A town was established in 1881 for the construction of the Atchison, Topeka and Santa Fe Railway. Named after T. Jefferson Coolidge, former president of the AT&SF Railway, it was a stockpile of railroad equipment and the last stop for paying travelers.

Starting in 1889, however, the railroad facilities were relocated to Gallup, leaving Coolidge an empty shell. During the Spanish-American War in 1898, the site became Dewey, in honor of the hero of Manila Bay, but two years later it was renamed Guam, in recognition of America's newest possession. Finally, when Route

66 became a reality in 1926, a new settlement of Coolidge was established, this time named in honor of President Calvin Coolidge.

The present interstate, which directly overlays the earlier Route 66 here, descends until it reaches Jamestown. Three miles west is the overpass and turnoff to the small Navajo community of Iyanbito (Buffalo Springs).

The dominant geological feature of this stretch of highway is the Red Rocks a couple of miles to the north. The floor of this broad valley and foundation for the cliffs is the Chinle Formation, laid down in the late Triassic Period. More than one hundred miles west, this same formation produced all the fossilized trees at Petrified Forest National Park. Throughout the Jurassic Period (135–180 million years ago), vast areas of sand dunes consolidated into the cross-bedded Entrada Sandstone. In an extensive lagoon that covered most of northwestern New Mexico, the gypsum and limestone of the Todilto Formation were precipitated. This salty basin was eventually overwhelmed by reddish sands and silts of the Summerville Formation, and covered over, in turn, by layers of wind-blown sands known as the Bluff Formation. The final Jurassic deposit, and the capstone layer for the Red Rocks, is the Morrison Formation, created by sandstones and siltstones deposited by streams and wind-blown sands.

In a couple of those canyons eroding out of the Red Rocks, almost in line with the overpass to both

The entrance to Fort Wingate Army Depot.

Fort Wingate and McGaffey Recreational Area (milepost 33), Troy Donahue, as Lieutenant Matt Hazard, defeated a large war party of Apaches in Raoul Walsh's 1964 classic film, *A Distant Trumpet*. To the left are fields with more than a thousand concrete, earth-covered ordnance storage facilities, locally referred to as "igloos," at Fort Wingate.

Initially established as Fort Fauntleroy in August 1860, the name was changed to Fort Lyon in September, 1861. However, by December both Fort Defiance (northwest of present-day Gallup) and Fort Lyon were abandoned and their garrisons assigned to the Albuquerque area because of the threat of a Confederate invasion from Texas.

After the Navajos were allowed to return to their ancestral homeland following the 1864 Long Walk and captivity, in 1868 the facilities at Fort Lyon were refurbished and renamed Fort Wingate.

In December 1918, the Army Ordnance Department took command of the military reservation. Storage areas were constructed for excess munitions being returned from Europe after the war. In 1925, the grounds containing the old fort were transferred to the Bureau of Indian Affairs for use as a boarding school for Navajo and Zuni children.

Between 1942 and 1945, hundreds of Navajos worked with Army personnel to produce munitions and artillery shells for the World War II war effort. And the Navajo Code Talkers were inducted here. By 1990, the ammunition began to be disposed of,

and by 1995 Fort Wingate Ordnance Depot was decommissioned by the U.S. Army.

Getting back to the Fort Wingate and McGaffey Recreational Area overpass, a westbound traveler can also drive onto the frontage road. This access road goes all the way into Gallup, and is the original Route 66. If you take this route, you will come to

the small Navajo community of Church Rock. This was built to house the Navajos and their families who were working at the Wingate Ordnance Depot during World War II.

Just to the north of Church Rock is a natural cave, with a spring, in the Red Rock cliffs. Commonly known as Kit Carson's Cave, it was one of several local sites where the first movie about Billy the Kid was made, King Vidor's 1930 epic, *Billy The Kid*, starring John Mack Brown and Wallace Beery.

Adjacent to the Church Rock community, but

Zuni Olla Maidens balance pottery on their heads in the Inter-Tribal Indian Ceremonial parade held in Gallup during the month of August.

Overleaf: The Red Rock Balloon Rally is a very colorful and scenic event with more than 150 balloons every year.

Below: A young crowned princess rides and smiles to the crowd in the Inter-Tribal Indian Ceremonial parade.

featuring the majestic rock formation known as "Church Rock," is the Red Rock Park. Nestled in a picturesque canyon, the facility includes a public campground and a century-old trading post. There is also an excellent foot trail to the top of Pyramid Rock, the highest point in the park.

Major activities at the park include the annual Gallup Inter-Tribal Indian Ceremonial festivities during the second weekend in August, the annual colorful Red Rock Balloon Rally held the first weekend in December, and several top-notch rodeos throughout the summer. As you continue west on the original Route 66, the Navajo-owned Fire Rock Casino comes into view. But just before that, you will drive over the same road that was driven by the Joad family in the 1940 John Ford production of *The Grapes of Wrath.*

After the Civil War, a stage route following the 35th Parallel North was established from Santa Fe to Los Angeles. Known as the Emigrant Trail, it served as a route for wagon trains, military expeditions, and stagecoaches. Just west of Fort Wingate, a stage-coach station and the Blue Goose Saloon catered to the needs of travelers, as well as any thirsty local coal miners and soldiers.

In the spring of 1881, the Atlantic & Pacific Railroad (now the Burlington Northern and Santa Fe Railway) constructed their railway westward along the route of the old trail. The railroad paymaster, David Gallup, put his office near the Blue Goose Saloon, and the Blue Goose quickly had some competition—twenty-two saloons, two dance halls, and a lot of tents!

The name "Gallup" stuck, and in 1889 the railroad began moving their division offices from Coolidge to Gallup. When it was incorporated as a town in 1891, it also boasted a school, a couple of churches, rows of nice homes, and several mercantile and grocery stores along Front Street. This site was chosen for a railroad community in part because of the abundance of coal. Coal was necessary for the steam engines at the time, and by the mid-'90s, over a dozen major coal mines were in full production.

H-1892   EL NAVAJO, FRED HARVEY HOTEL, GALLUP, NEW MEXICO (AFTER PAINTING BY FRED GEARY)

The coal mines, railroad, and mercantile operations brought in a continuous flow of workers, primarily from southern Europe (Slavic and Italian), Mexico and, within the past fifteen years or so, Palestine and the Arabian Peninsula. And from the beginning, the local workforce included a number of Navajos, Zunis, and members of Laguna Pueblo.

Once it was determined that the major road would run through Gallup, the local leaders and merchants aggressively pursued tourism. Although it took more than a decade of constant road improvements, as well as improvements to autos and buses, tourism was still mainly associated with the railroad.

In 1923, the Fred Harvey Company opened a monumental hotel in Gallup. The initial plans for El Navajo Hotel were laid out by Harvey's architectural designer, Mary Elizabeth Jane Colter. Working with her boss, John Huckel, Colter created the interior designs, motifs, and furnishings, and conceived of an overall decor based on Navajo sandpaintings, a first for public building interior design. With the consultation of Navajo medicine men, authentic sandpaintings were added to walls throughout the building. This magnificent structure, with its front facade facing the railroad, was dedicated on May 26, 1923, with thirty Navajo medicine men and over two thousand other people in attendance. After World War II, however, there was a tremendous increase in auto traffic, and a corresponding reduction in passenger trains. The beautiful El Navajo Hotel was demolished in July, 1957, to make way for expanding Route 66 into four lanes through Gallup. What was originally Front Street, and then for awhile, Railroad Avenue, is now officially listed as "Historic 66 Avenue."

The railroad depot has now been remodeled into the Gallup Cultural Center. It is maintained by the Southwest Indian Foundation and contains a museum and information center.

By the mid-'30s, Gallup was also nurturing a love affair with the film industry. Several motion picture companies had already come into the area, as well as into Monument Valley on the Arizona-Utah border on the Navajo Reservation.

Ron Griffith, brother of the well-known movie producer, D. W. Griffith, designed and supervised the construction of "The World's Largest Ranch House," the El Rancho Hotel, on the east side of Gallup. This 3-story, 110-room hotel was built to accommodate the lavish lifestyles of Hollywood celebrities who stayed there while filming, mostly Westerns, in this part of New Mexico. Following the grand opening on December 17, 1937, names that appeared on the guest register included Spencer Tracy, Humphrey Bogart, John Wayne, Errol Flynn, Ida Lupino, Katharine Hepburn, Burt Lancaster, Rita Hayworth, Gregory Peck, Kirk Douglas, and Ronald Reagan.

But in the 1960s, as Westerns faded, El Rancho faded as well. The last major Western filmed locally, and using El Rancho as an actors' residence, was John Sturges's 1965 film, *The Hallelujah Trail*. After twenty years of neglect, the facilities were purchased and restored by trader Armand Ortega. Since its reopening in May, 1988, the original ambience of the rooms, restaurant, 49er lounge, and lobby reflect that wonderful period of Route 66.

Left: Mary Elizabeth Jane Colter's Fred Harvey creation, El Navajo Hotel.

Below: The interior of the El Rancho Hotel is a feast for the eyes.

On the south side of Historic 66 Avenue, the business district offers a multitude of Native American arts and crafts outlets. Good selections of Pueblo pottery, Navajo textiles, Hopi carvings, and jewelry produced by several Southwest tribes can be found at Silver Dust, Indian Touch, First American Traders, Desert Dove, Red Shell Jewelry, and especially at the several storefronts that constitute Richardson's Trading Post. Check out the Eagle Café and the Rex Museum as well. A block south, on Coal Avenue, one can find many more Indian arts and crafts retail outlets, an excellent moccasin shop, several restaurants, and the historic El Morro Theater.

Above: El Rancho Hotel was a favorite among movie stars.

Right: Bill Richardson, owner of Richardson's Trading Post in Gallup.

Gallup has been called the Indian Capital of the World. There are Indian schools, hospitals, and agencies here. The government agencies connected to the Native American populations are among the biggest employers in the area. Indians are a big part of the business of Gallup. And every night, between Memorial Day and Labor Day, beginning at 7:00 p.m., there are Indian dances in the County Court House plaza, free to the public.

Both 2nd Street and the Munoz overpass Route 602 connect south of town, and continue to Zuni Pueblo and El Morro National Monument.

In June, you can also participate in a major event sponsored by the New Mexico Route 66 Association: the annual New Mexico Motor Tour, which starts in Gallup and ends in Tucumcari. Experience New Mexico highway travel as it was in the 1940s, '50s, and '60s. Participants can make the cruise in a classic or contemporary car, travel trailer, or motorcycle. The cruise always ends with a banquet in the terminal city.

Continuing on Historic 66, you'll find the USA RV Park on the west side of Gallup. The business is operated by John Moore, one of the most avid supporters of the Route 66 legacy. It's a neat place to spend the night, and his gift shop is extensive.

Hopi dancers in the Gallup Inter-Tribal Indian Ceremonial parade.

Right: Meet Lil' Miss Eastern Navajo, Kyla Bitsie!

Below: Bull riding at the Inter-Tribal Ceremonial rodeo.

Continuing west past the truck stop, Historic 66 Avenue becomes State Route 118, which basically follows the original Route 66 all the way to the Arizona state line. The road switches over to the south side of the interstate at the truck weigh station, but then crosses over to the north side as you approach the Manuelito Chapter House (Navajo) and school.

A couple of miles farther west is the famous Miller Cave off to the right. The cave, now closed to the public, was prominent in 1951 when a large Ancestral Puebloan–looking ruin was fabricated in the cave and used in the motion picture *Ace in the Hole*, which was produced by Billy Wilder and starred Kirk Douglas and Jan Sterling.

In 1958, MGM Studios filmed scenes in the surrounding hills and mesas, as well as at this slightly used Ancestral Puebloan site when they produced *Fort Massacre.*

Just beyond the ruins of the Mike Kirk Trading Post, the road skirts Devil's Cliff. Rocks keep dislodging from the cliff surface and fall on the road, much to the consternation of travelers.

Fort Chief Yellowhorse and several trading posts also under the Yellowhorse name await the traveler in the small assortment of cafés, garages, truck stops, and tourist-related businesses that compose Lupton.

Welcome to Arizona!

Side Trip

ZUNI AND EL MORRO NATIONAL MONUMENT

Start at Exit 20 in Gallup. Historic 66 can access the overpass going south. This is also the beginning of State Highway 602. If you're on 2nd Street and going south, a stop at the Perry Null Trading Post is strongly suggested. For many years it was operated by one of the most respected traders in Gallup history, Tobe Turpen.

Second Street connects with Highway 602 south of town and goes to two more trading posts: Joe Milo's at VanDerWagen, seventeen miles south of Gallup, and Winfield's Trading Post just a few miles farther down the road. Shortly after leaving Winfield's, the highway enters the Zuni Reservation.

Turn right on Highway 53 and go eight miles to the Pueblo of Zuni. At the Zuni Visitor Center you can find out the local events and acquaint yourself with the visitor rules and regulations regarding the pueblo. Similar to Isleta, Acoma, and Laguna, Zuni Pueblo residents cherish their privacy, and when you tour the historic part of Zuni, always remember that you are their guest and conduct yourself accordingly. The Zuni Visitor Center, for a fee, conducts periodic guided tours to the old part of the pueblo, to the mission (built in 1629), and out to the Hawikku (or Hawikuh) ruins. They also provide maps to studios of Zuni potters, silversmiths, and other craftspeople.

The Cities of Cibola

Human occupation of this region has existed for the past seven thousand years at least. By three thousand years ago, cultural characteristics of what has become known as the Ancestral Pueblo society began to appear—people congregated in small villages and practiced rudimentary agriculture. Gradually, this culture not only survived this inhospitable environment but progressed in architecture, farming techniques, religious practices, and the methods of making pottery.

By the early 1100s, the people living in the Zuni River–Little Colorado River drainages began to organize their communities around a large ceremonial structure called a "great kiva." The Village of the Great Kivas along the Nutria River is one example of this type of community center. These centers were organized into a large regional trade and exchange system, focusing on Chaco Canyon to the north. But in the late 1100s, the people traded with people living along the Mogollon Rim to the south.

By AD 1250, the settlement pattern had changed as people aggregated into large, well-planned pueblos. At one point there were thirty-six large multistoried pueblos in this region, but then during the 1300s, for reasons not completely understood, the Ancestral Pueblo population decreased, and many large communal buildings were vacated.

During the 1400s, people with a Mogollon cultural tradition migrated into the area. A new culture and language, a composite of Ancestral Pueblo and Mogollon cultural traits, began to emerge. These people, the A:sh'iwi', settled along the Zuni River, where extensive agriculture could be practiced. Six pueblos were occupied during the 1500s. Besides agriculture, bison hunting remained important to their tradition and economy, especially in the trading of hides to their southern neighbors.

The six villages were named Kyaki':ma, Mats'a:kya, Halona:wa, Kwa'kin'a, Kechiba:wa, and Hawikku. This cluster of villages became known throughout the region by the trade item they specialized in, bison hides (not gold). The Zuni word for bison is "Shi'wona" often pronounced "Cibola."

Ever mindful of the old Spanish legend of the Seven Cities of Antilia, and similar tales of a wealthy cluster of cities in a place called Cibola, the Viceroy of New Spain (Mexico), Antonio de Mendoza, dispatched the Franciscan priest Fray Marcos de Niza to investigate these reports. Fray Marcos and a contingent of Natives, with the black slave Estevan as the guide, left Compostela in March, 1539. When he returned six months later without Estevan (who had been killed by the Cibolanos), he had an incredible story to tell. Although his reports and observations turned out to be fairly factual, the Spanish authorities chose to read into them only what they wanted to hear.

Consequently, the greatest exploration undertaken in the New World was launched under the leadership of Don Francisco Vázquez de Coronado—and the destination was the fabled Seven Golden Cities of Cibola. CONTINUED ➤

WIKIMEDIA COMMONS

Coronado Sets Out to the North by Frederic Remington, 1861–1909.

Right: Juanita Edaakie, of the Zuni Olla Maidens, participates in the traditional dancing group of close relatives that perform throughout New Mexico, in the East Coast cities, and Canada.

On July 7, 1540, Coronado and his seventy mounted soldiers arrived at Hawikku. When Pueblo leaders refused to give Coronado access, the Spaniards attacked and took control of the town. Thus, a 300-year relationship, often hostile, began between the Spaniards and Native American tribes of the Southwest. Following the Pueblo Revolt of 1680, and throughout the Spanish reconquest during the 1690s, five Zuni villages were abandoned as survivors consolidated people and resources into one village for security and survival.

Beginning in the 1700s, the Zuni population has occupied the ancient site of Halona:wa, or, as it is usually spelled today, Halona. Today, Zuni is the largest of New Mexico's nineteen pueblos, with a reservation of nearly seven hundred square miles and a population of around 11,000. It is one of the most traditional pueblos, with a unique language, culture, and history. Perhaps 80 percent of the families create art or craft items, and they are famous for their silver and turquoise inlay jewelry or cluster work, stone fetish carvings, and pottery.

Visitors can tour the A:shiwi A:wan museum and heritage center; The Inn at Halona, a combination restaurant and bed-and-breakfast inn; Pueblo of Zuni Arts & Crafts store; the old mission; Our Lady of Guadalupe Church; the eagle and raptor aviary; and the Turquoise Village Trading Post.

The Zuni calendar is marked by a cycle of traditional ceremonial activities that culminate with the annual Sha'la'k'o observance in early December. Other events include the annual Main Street Festival in early May, the Ancient Way Arts Festival on Memorial Day weekend, the Zuni Arts & Crafts Fair in August (coincides with the Ceremonial Days in Gallup), and the Ancient Way Fall Festival on the first weekend in October.

El Morro National Monument

Heading out of Zuni, go east on Highway 53 and retrace your route to the junction with Highway 602. At this point, you can go back to Gallup by turning left, or you can continue on Highway 53 and arrive nineteen miles later at the tree-shaded Mormon farming community of Ramah. Thirteen miles after Ramah, you come to the entrance drive to El Morro National Monument. The Visitor Center has informational items and a small museum.

Inscription Rock is a large sandstone promontory with a pool of water at its base. About seven hundred years ago, two Zuni/Ancestral Puebloan villages were located on the cliff top. One of them, A'ts'ina, has been partially excavated. The two-mile round-trip Mesa Top Trail entails some vigorous climbing, but the A'ts'ina ruins and the panoramic views are worth it. The Inscription Rock Trail is an easier half-mile paved loop that takes you to the pool of water and along the base of the cliff where there are hundreds of carvings and inscriptions. The earliest human and animal petroglyphs were carved by the residents of these villages. For centuries, campers left evidence of their Cibola-Acoma trail passage—symbols, names, dates, and

inscriptions register the cultures and history of this fascinating section of the Southwest. "Paso por aqui"—the earliest Spanish inscription—is by Juan de Oñate in 1605, and the last American inscription is dated 1881, the year the Atlantic & Pacific Railroad worked its way into Gallup. With the coming of the railroad twenty-five miles to the north, this ancient trace past El Morro became obsolete as a long-distance thoroughfare.

When Congress passed the Antiquities Act in 1906, it created the authority of the president to establish National Monuments. In spite of its remote location, El Morro's historic importance was well known. In December 1906, President Theodore Roosevelt designated it as the nation's second national monument.

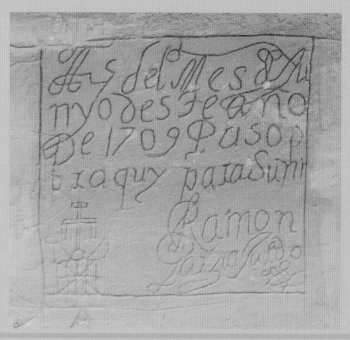

Top and above: Travelers through history left messages on Inscription Rock at El Morro National Monument.

Right: Atsinna Pueblo, the largest at El Morro National Monument, had 875 rooms.

Night falls on the Santo Domingo Trading Post.

ACKNOWLEDGMENTS

I am grateful to the many folks I met along my travels for their various help and friendship. Special thanks go to Vickie Ashcraft, Andy House, John Moore, Richard and Gail Talley, and Tom Willis for sharing their time and knowledge. Thanks also to Larry Lindahl for his tenacity and ability to get great photos.

—MARTIN LINK

At the top of any list is my wife, Wendy, whose encouragement, understanding, and patience during my many trips was heaven sent. Next up is the winning team at Rio Nuevo Publishers: Ross Humphreys, Aaron Downey, Jim Turner, and book designer David Jenney.

While photographing the people and places along Route 66 in New Mexico, I met many generous folks that I wish to thank. Along the way these people contributed their time, expertise, or a comfortable room that made completing the journey possible.

The names are listed by city, traveling east to west. *Tucumcari*: Gail and Richard Talley, owners, Motel Safari; and Paula J. Neese, Tucumcari Historical Museum. *Santa Rosa*: Mike and Colleen Gallegos, owners, La Mesa Motel; James "Bozo" and Anna Cordova, owners, Route 66 Auto Museum.

Moriarty: Archie and Beth Lewis, owners, Lewis Antique Auto & Toy Museum. *Edgewood*: Roger Alink, founder, Wildlife West Nature Park. *Albuquerque*: Heather Briganti, Senior Communications & Tourism Manager of Albuquerque; Steve and Kathy Hiatt, owners, Bottger Mansion of Old Town; Joe Dan Lowry, curator and owner, Turquoise Museum, and son Jacob Lowry; Bob Myers, Director, American International Rattlesnake Museum; and Kimberly Preston, waitress (model), 66 Diner. *Corrales*: Denise Stramel & Keith Buderus, owners, The Chocolate Turtle Bed & Breakfast. *Santa Fe*: Maggie Elliot, for your generous hospitality; Dawn Aley, owner of the 1953 Chevrolet pickup truck (and model) photographed at Santo Domingo Trading Post, plus owner of Silver Saddle Motel; and Miguel Valdivia (driver in trading post photo). *Santo Domingo Pueblo*: Mona Angel, Tribal Planner, Tribal Policy & Community Development; and Patrick A. Bailon, Santo Domingo Trading Post Renovation Project Coordinator. *Grants*: Steve Owen, volunteer, Western New Mexico Aviation Heritage Museum. *Gallup*: Ken Riege, general manager, Comfort Suites Gallup; Susan Oldenburg (from Albuquerque), "J.A.M." hot air balloon pilot at the Red Rock Balloon Rally; and author Martin Link.

—LARRY LINDAHL

The 66 Diner in Albuquerque
serves it up just like the old days.

PLACES TO SEE ALONG NEW MEXICO'S ROUTE 66

CHAPTER 2
GLENRIO TO SANTA ROSA

Blue Swallow Motel
815 East Route 66 Boulevard
Tucumcari, NM 88401
(575) 461-9849
http://blueswallowmotel.com/

Mesalands Community College's Dinosaur Museum and Natural Science Laboratory
222 East Laughlin Street
Tucumcari, NM 88401
(575) 461-3466
www.mesalands.edu/community/dinosaur-museum/

Motel Safari
722 Route 66
Tucumcari, NM 88401
(575) 461-1048
www.themotelsafari.com

New Mexico Route 66 Museum
PO Box 66
Tucumcari, NM 88401
www.nmrt66museum.org
(575) 461-1694

Russell's Truck & Travel Center
1583 Frontage Road 4132
Glenrio, NM 88434
(575) 576-8700
www.russellsttc.com

Tee Pee Curios
924 Route 66
Tucumcari, NM 88401
(575) 461-3773

Tucumcari Historical Museum
416 South Adams Street
Tucumcari, NM 88401
(575) 461-4201
www.cityoftucumcari.com/museum

CHAPTER 2 SIDE TRIP
FORT SUMNER

Billy the Kid Museum
1435 East Sumner Avenue
Fort Sumner, NM 88119
(575) 355-2380
www.billythekidmuseumfortsumner.com/

Fort Sumner State Monument
3647 Billy the Kid Road
Fort Sumner, NM 88119
(575) 355-2573

Old Fort Days
(575) 355-7705

Old Fort Sumner Museum
3501 Billy The Kid Road
Fort Sumner, NM 88119
(575) 355-2942

CHAPTER 3
SANTA ROSA TO TIJERAS CANYON

Blue Hole
1085 Blue Hole Road
Santa Rosa, NM 88435
(575) 472-3763

City of Natural Lakes
(575) 472-3110

La Mesa Motel
2415 Route 66
Santa Rosa, NM 88435
(575) 472-3021

Lewis Antique Auto and Toy Museum
905 Route 66
Moriarty, NM 87035
(505) 832-6131

Route 66 Auto Museum
2866 Route 66
Santa Rosa, NM 88435
(575) 472-1966

Whiting Brothers Service Station, Sal Lucero
Moriarty, NM
(505) 832-4202

CHAPTER 3 SIDE TRIP
SANTA FE

Georgia O'Keeffe Museum
217 Johnson Street
Santa Fe, NM 87501
(505) 490-6753
www.okeeffemuseum.org

La Fonda on the Plaza
100 E San Francisco Street
Santa Fe, NM 87501
(505) 982-5511
www.lafondasantafe.com

Loretto Chapel
207 Old Santa Fe Trail
Santa Fe, NM 87501
(505) 982-0092
www.lorettochapel.com

Museum of Indian Arts & Culture
708 Camino Lejo
Santa Fe, NM 87505
(505) 476-1250

Museum of International Folk Art
706 Camino Lejo
Santa Fe, NM 87505
(505) 476-1200
www.internationalfolkart.org

Museum of New Mexico
725 Camino Lejo
Santa Fe, NM 87505
(505) 476-1125
www.museumofnewmexico.org

Museum of Spanish Colonial Art
750 Camino Lejo
Santa Fe, NM 87505
(505) 982-4585
http://spanishcolonial.org/museum

**New Mexico History Museum
and Palace of the Governors**
105 West Palace Avenue
Santa Fe, NM 87501
(505) 476-5200

New Mexico Museum of Art
107 West Palace Avenue
Santa Fe, NM 87501
(505) 476-5072

NPS Route 66 Preservation Program
(505) 988-6701)
http://ncptt.nps.gov/rt66

Pecos National Historic Park
Pecos, NM
(505) 757-7241
www.nps.gov/peco/index.htm

Santa Fe Chamber of Commerce
1644 Saint Michaels Drive
Santa Fe, NM 87505
(505) 983-7317

Santa Fe Fiesta
(505) 204-1598
www.santafefiesta.org

Santa Fe Indian Market
215 Washington Avenue
Santa Fe, NM 87501
(505) 984-6760
(505) 983-5220
www.swaia.org

Santa Fe Opera
301 Opera Drive
Santa Fe, NM 87506
(505) 982-3851
(505) 986-5900
www.santafeopera.org

Silver Saddle Motel
2810 Cerrillos Road
Santa Fe, NM 87507
(505) 471-7663

Spanish Market
750 Camino Lejo
Santa Fe, NM 87505
(505) 982-2226
http://spanishcolonial.org/this-is-spanish-
market

Wheelwright Museum of the American Indian
704 Camino Lejo
Santa Fe, NM 87505
(505) 982-4636
https://wheelwright.org

CHAPTER 4
ALBUQUERQUE

**Anderson-Abruzzo Albuquerque International
Balloon Museum**
9201 Balloon Museum Drive Northeast
Albuquerque, NM 87113
(505) 880-0500
www.balloonmuseum.com

American International Rattlesnake Museum
202 San Felipe NW, Suite A
Albuquerque, NM 87104
(505) 242-6569
www.rattlesnakes.com

66 Diner
1405 Central Avenue
Albuquerque, NM 87106
(505) 247-1421
www.66diner.com

Balloon Fiesta Park
Balloon Fiesta Parkway Northeast
Albuquerque, NM 87113
(888) 422-7277
www.balloonfiesta.com

Bottger Mansion of Old Town
110 San Felipe Street Northwest
Albuquerque, NM 87104
(505) 243-3639
www.bottger.com

Celtic Festival, Jay Vandersloot
(505) 362-1733
www.celtfestabq.com

Enchanted Trails RV Park
14305 Central Avenue Northwest
Albuquerque, NM 87121
(800)-326-6317
(505)-831-6317
www.enchantedtrails.com

Indian Pueblo Cultural Center
(505) 843-7270

International Balloon Fiesta
(888) 422-7277
www.balloonfiesta.com

Isleta Hotel & Casino
11000 Broadway Boulevard Southeast
Albuquerque, NM 87105
(505) 724-3800
www.isleta.com

Isleta Eagle Golf Club
4001 Highway 47 Southeast
Albuquerque, NM 87105
(505) 848.1900
www.isleta.com

Isleta Lakes and RV Park
4051 Highway 47 Southeast
Albuquerque, NM 87105
(505) 244-8102

Maxwell Museum of Anthropology
1 University Boulevard Northeast
Albuquerque, NM 87131
(505) 277-4404
www.unm.edu/~maxwell

Museum of Southwestern Biology
1 University Boulevard Northeast
Albuquerque, NM 87131
(505) 277-5340
https://msb.unm.edu

National Museum of Nuclear Science & History
601 Eubank
Albuquerque, NM 87123
(505) 245-2137
www.nuclearmuseum.org

New Mexico Route 66 Association
14305 Central Avenue Northwest
Albuquerque, NM 87121
(505) 385-1410
www.rt66nm.org

New Mexico State Fairgrounds
300 San Pedro Drive Northeast
Albuquerque, NM 87108
(505) 265-1791
http://statefair.exponm.com

Petroglyph National Monument
6510 Western Trail Northwest
Albuquerque, NM 87120
(505) 839-4429
www.nps.gov/petr/index.htm

Sandia Peak Tram Office
10 Tramway Loop Northeast
Albuquerque, NM 87122
(505) 857-8977
(505) 298-8518
www.sandiapeak.com

Tinkertown Museum
121 Sandia Crest Road
Sandia Park NM 87047
(505) 281-5233
www.tinkertown.com

Turquoise Museum
2107 Central Avenue Northwest
Albuquerque, NM 87104
(505) 247-8650
www.turquoisemuseum.com

University of New Mexico Art Museum
1 University of New Mexico
Albuquerque, NM 87131
(505) 277-4001
http://unmartmuseum.org

Unser Racing Museum
1776 Montaño Road Northwest
Los Ranchos de Albuquerque, NM 87107
(505) 341-1776
www.unserracingmuseum.com

CHAPTER 4 SIDE TRIP
LOS LUNAS

Isleta Pueblo
(505) 869-3111
www.isletapueblo.com

Luna Mansion Landmark Steakhouse
110 West Main Street
Los Lunas, NM 87031
(505) 865-7333
info@lunamansion.com

National Hispanic Cultural Center
1701 4th Street Southwest
Albuquerque, NM 87102
(505) 246-2261
www.nationalhispaniccenter.org

CHAPTER 5
ALBUQUERQUE TO MCCARTYS

Kasha-Katuwe Tent Rocks National Monument
Cochiti, NM 87072
(505) 761-8700
www.blm.gov/nm/st/en/prog/NLCS/KKTR_NM.html

Route 66 Casino Hotel
14500 Central Avenue Southwest
Albuquerque, NM 87121
(505) 352-7866
www.rt66casino.com

Sky City Casino
(888) 759-2489
www.skycity.com/alpha.html

CHAPTER 5 SIDE TRIP
ACOMA PUEBLO

Sky City Cultural Center/Haak'u Museum
Haaku Road
Acoma Pueblo, NM 87034
(800) 747-0181

CHAPTER 6
MCCARTYS TO THE
CONTINENTAL DIVIDE

Cibola Arts Council/ Double Six Gallery
1001 W Santa Fe Aveue
Grants, NM 87020
(505) 287-7311
http://cibolaartscouncil.com

**Western New Mexico Aviation
Heritage Museum**
Grants-Milan Municipal Airport
Grants, NM 87020
www.cibolahistory.org/aviation-
heritage-museum.html

CHAPTER 6 SIDE TRIP
CHACO CULTURE
NATIONAL HISTORICAL PARK

Chaco Culture National Historical Park
(505) 786-7014
www.nps.gov/chcu/index.htm

CHAPTER 7
CONTINENTAL DIVIDE TO LUPTON

Bill Malone Trading
235 West Coal Avenue
Gallup, NM 87301
(505) 863-3401

Butler's Office Equipment & Supply
1900 Route 66 #3
Gallup, NM 87301
(505) 722-6661
www.butlersofficecity.com

El Rancho Hotel
1000 East 66
Gallup, NM 87301
(505) 863-9311
www.elranchohotel.com

Ellis Tanner Trading Company
1980 Highway 602
Gallup, NM 87301
(505) 863-4434
www.etanner.com

Gallup Cultural Center
201 East Highway 66
Gallup, NM 87301
(505) 863-4131
www.southwestindian.com/foundation/
cultural-center

Richardson's Trading Company
222 West Historic Highway 66
Gallup, NM 87301
(505) 722-4762
www.richardsontrading.com

USA RV Park
2925 West Historic 66 Avenue
Gallup, NM 87301
(505) 863-5021
www.usarvpark.com

CHAPTER 7 SIDE TRIP
ZUNI AND EL MORRO
NATIONAL MONUMENT

El Morro National Monument
Ramah, NM 87321
(505) 783-4226
www.nps.gov/elmo/index.htm

Joe Milo's Trading Post
NM-602
Vanderwagen, NM 87326
(888) 563-6456
www.joemilo.com

Perry Null Trading Post
1710 South 2nd Street
Gallup, NM 87301
(505) 863-5249
www.perrynulltrading.com

Winfield's Trading Post
1811 State Highway 602
Vanderwagen, NM 87301
(505) 778-5544
www.winfieldtradingcompany.com

Zuni Visitor Center
PO Box 339
Zuni, NM 87327
(505) 782-7239
www.zunitourism.com

NANCY WADE

MARTIN LINK graduated from the University of Arizona in 1958 and has devoted his life experiences to the archaeology and history of our Southwest. His numerous publications include *Navajo: A Century of Progress, 1868–1968*, *The Goat in the Rug*, and *Navajo Country Pioneers*. For 18 years he was the publisher of *The Indian Trader* newspaper. Martin lives in Gallup, New Mexico.

NINA REHFELD

LARRY LINDAHL is an award-winning travel and landscape photographer whose work appears in books including *Ancient Southwest* (Rio Nuevo Publishers), *Arizona Kicks on Route 66* (Rio Nuevo Publishers), and *Lasting Light: 125 Years of Grand Canyon Photography* (Cooper Square Publishing). He is also the author and photographer of *Secret Sedona: Sacred Moments in the Landscapes* (Arizona Highways Books). His work is frequently published in magazines and calendars, and is displayed in several permanent exhibits. Larry lives in